Also by Kevin Nelson

Baseball's Greatest Quotes
Baseball's Greatest Insults
The Greatest Stories Ever Told About Baseball

A FIRESIDE BOOK

Published by Simon & Schuster

New York   London   Toronto

Sydney   Tokyo

Singapore

THE GREATEST GOLF SHOT EVER MADE

*and other lively and entertaining
tales from the lore and
history of golf*

by Kevin Nelson

Illustrations by Sheila Nelson

F

FIRESIDE

Simon & Schuster Building
Rockefeller Center
1230 Avenue of the Americas
New York, New York 10020

Designed by Liney Li
Manufactured in the United States of America

10 9 8 7 6 5 4 3 2 1

Library of Congress Cataloging in Publication Data

Nelson, Kevin, date.
    The greatest golf shot ever made : and other lively and
entertaining tales from the lore and history of golf / by Kevin
Nelson : illustrations by Sheila Nelson.
        p.   cm.
    1. Golf—History.   I. Title.
GV963.N45   1992
796.352—dc20   91-28291
                                                                        CIP
ISBN 0-671-73225-0

Dedicated to Ralph Van Pool, Kevin McNamara, Bill Armbruster, Abel Kessler, and all the other golfers I played with during the making of this book

Contents

Contents

Contents

13

Preface

The original premise of this book was to collect all of the great stories of golf and put them under one roof. This, it was discovered, may well be an impossible task. People have been playing golf for hundreds of years, and telling stories about it for just as long. Nevertheless, many, many, many of the game's best stories are contained in this volume.

Also included are a number of the author's own opinions, observations, and unrepentant heresies. These opinions are solely the author's and he takes full pride and responsibility for them. Like the stories, their intent is to entertain, enlighten, and amuse.

A book of this kind would seem to have the most value to a newcomer to golf, someone who is only beginning to appreciate the intricacies of this great game and may not know much about its richly varied history and lore. But I think even old hands at the game will derive some benefit and entertainment from the tales told herein. I once took a lesson from a pro who was unclear who Harry Vardon was, and which grip he used. To play golf and not know about Vardon—or Bobby Jones or Babe Zaharias or even nervous Leo Diegel—is to miss a great deal of the pleasure the game affords.

The book proceeds, very loosely, on a historical framework, starting with the time hundreds of years ago when golf was played by kings and noblemen and extending to the Faldos and Normans of the contemporary era, the current kings of the game. Having said that, I would not recommend reading from front to back in the normal manner, but rather dipping in wherever you like, according to what suits your fancy.

This book owes much to many people, not least of whom are the writers who have made the literature of golf unsurpassed in all of sports. Many thanks also to Maureen O'Rourke, for her under-standing; Gene Brissie, for his idea; Angela Miller, for her eye for talent; Kara Leverte, for her expert guidance; and Sheila and Annie, for being themselves.

—Kevin Nelson

Part One

THE
ROYAL AND
ANCIENT GAME

The origins of golf, Ben Hogan's bad dream, what Domingo Lopez has in common with King James, how Francis became a hero, and other amusing and fascinating tales of a historical, yet timely, nature

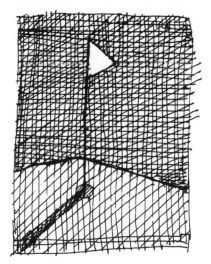

The Origins of Golf

It may come as a surprise to some to learn that golf was invented by men tending sheep in the fields of Scotland. It was a game they played with their walking sticks, or staffs. The ball they used was an ordinary rock they found on the ground. And the hole—the target they aimed for—was perhaps a rabbit's hole, like what Alice disappeared into.

Men, with sticks, hitting rocks into a rabbit's hole. This, of course, is the legend of how the game started, and most golf historians, who have their own theories about golf's origins, debunk it.

But with all the complications in golf today—all the money involved, the formidable if not overbearing corporate presence on the pro circuits, the controversies over opening up country clubs to blacks and women, the influx of new technology and the unyielding emphasis on stroke and technique, the booming popularity of the game coupled with dawdling slow play and the near impossibility of getting tee times on many courses—given all this, it is somehow comforting to keep this image of shepherds and sticks and rocks in mind. As devilishly difficult as it is to play, as maddeningly frustrating as it can be, golf is, at bottom, a simple game.

Old Harry's Everlasting Grip

Certainly, you don't need to know the lore and history of golf to play the game and enjoy it. It's a game you play—that's its chief appeal. Get some sticks, maybe pick up a copy of *Golf: My Way* for a few pointers, and go out and do it.

One of the drawbacks with this approach, though, is that you might not notice the old man standing behind you as you hit.

There he is.

Oh, no, you turned too slowly. He's gone now.

Ah, but he's come back. You can't keep him away for long. He does so enjoy the game. Do you see him yet? No?

The old man's name is Harry Vardon. The name may vaguely ring a bell, but probably not. He's been dead an awfully long time. Harry was a Britisher, in the days around the turn of the century when Britain ruled golf. Then widely acknowledged as the world's best player, he made his first trip to America in 1900, and he may have done more to popularize the game in its infancy here than any other person. He was a virtuoso with the long irons, working the ball around the course as if it were radar controlled. It was said that Harry was such an accurate ball-striker that after playing a round he would come back the next day and hit his shots into the divots he had created the day before. His putting was not up to these standards, but as one writer remarked, "Vardon gave himself less putting to do than any other man."

Vardon won the 1900 U.S. Open in a cakewalk, but this was considered no great feat. The big tournament of the day was the British Open—Harry won six of them—while America was a backwater stop of little significance in the golfing cosmos. Many other things have changed since then. Vardon carried only seven or eight wood-shafted clubs, and people used such funny names as "mashie" and "niblick" to describe them. Harry wore a hard collar and tie and tightly buttoned jacket on the golf course, and it's hard to imagine how anyone could make a full swing dressed in such a getup as that. This was the era, too, of the gutta-percha ball—a relic of the nineteenth century—although Vardon was one of the few golfers to make a successful transition to this century's rubber-cored ball. He won his last two British Opens using a ball not unlike the ones we play with now.

Old Harry's game was adaptable because his swing was so fluid and easy. So fluid, in fact, that he often hit with a pipe in his mouth. "The general impression of his swing was one of grace and simplicity," writes Robert Browning. You can trace a line beginning with Harry up through Byron Nelson and on to the smooth swingers of today. His swing represented a stylish break from the choppier motions of his predecessors. People everywhere copied it, and in this way the gospel of golf spread.

But Harry was a flesh-and-blood man, not just a building block in the dreary pseudoscientific analysis of the modern golf swing. After his initial trip to the States he suffered two near-fatal bouts of tuberculosis, both times being forced to enter a sanatorium to regain his vigor. In 1913 he came on a second golfing tour of the U.S., and here he had the good grace to lose to Francis Ouimet in that historic Open at Brookline, Massachusetts, and thus give another inadvertent boost to American golf. On that tour he was asked by a female questioner who was the best left-handed golfer he had ever seen. "Never saw one that was worth a damn," said Harry.

Though well liked by his fellow pros, he could be gruff and blunt spoken. In 1920, at age fifty, he returned to the U.S. again and came heartbreakingly close to winning the Open a second time, faltering under high winds on the last nine holes. In the qualifying rounds for the tournament he was paired with the young American phenom Bobby Jones. Only eighteen at the time, Jones wanted badly to make a good impression on the old master, but on the seventh hole at the Inverness Club in Toledo, his nerves got the better of him and he butchered an approach shot to the green. Embarrassed by his duff, Jones asked meekly if Vardon had ever seen such a poor golf shot. "No," replied Harry.

Vardon died in 1937 and is buried in Totteridge parish churchyard north of London. He might well have dropped into permanent obscurity were it not for the way he held a golf club—with the little pinkie of the right hand overlapping the forefinger of the left. Harry did not invent the "overlapping" grip—historians give the credit to someone else—but he was its chief advocate and popularizer in the early part of the century. Now, of course, almost everybody who plays golf seriously uses it. "Up to now we haven't found a grip that promotes as effective a union between the body and the club," writes Ben Hogan. "One of these days a better one may come along, but until it does, we've got to stick with this one." And until it does, we've got to stick with Old Harry, standing beside us and looking silently on each time we swing a golf club.

The Shoemaker and the Prince

People have been playing golf for five hundred years, well before the advent of televised skins matches, the Shearson Lehman Hutton Andy Williams Open, or square grooves. One of the charms of the old-, old-, old-, old-time game is its royal connection. For nearly two hundred years, from the beginning of the sixteenth century until toward the end of the seventeenth, the royal Stuart line of Scottish kings (and later, English kings) all whacked away at that little feather-stuffed orb, albeit with mixed results.

James II of Scotland, or "James of the Fiery Face," was the monarch who, in 1457, issued his much quoted edict against the playing of golf: "the futeball and golfe be utterly cryed downe and not to be used." The reason for this was that Scotland was then at war with England, and James was concerned that his subjects were spending too much time working on their short game rather than practicing for military combat. James was later killed when a cannon blew up in his fiery face during a battle.

At the dawn of the 1500s, King James IV ruled over Scotland. He might fairly be described as the first golfing king. A note in a ledger of the time describes how he went out one day with his "clubbes," as it was spelled. His great-grandson was James VI, who became king of both Scotland and England. This James had his own personal clubmaker and taught his sons how to play. One of his sons ascended to the British throne as Charles I and was out on the links with his clubbes when a messenger arrived to inform him that a rebellion had broken out in his realm. Some things can wait in this life, but one of them is not golf. Unfazed, Charles finished out his game before attending to the uprising.

An early woman golfer was Mary Queen of Scots, who caused a

scandal when, a few days after her husband was murdered (in a plot in which Mary might have been involved), she was seen in public lustily whacking the ball around the links. While golf was viewed as excellent recreation by the Scottish people, it was not considered proper form for a person in mourning. Mary was ultimately beheaded after leading a full life.

(A modern parallel to Mary's plight might be President George Bush, who, after announcing the American buildup of forces in the Middle East following the Iraqi invasion of Kuwait, insisted on remaining in Kennebunkport to play golf and engage in other sporting pastimes. Never has a golf vacation been as chastised as that one.)

James II—not he of the fiery face, but another one—was a golfing monarch of Ireland, Scotland, and England until being overthrown in 1688. Before becoming king, James, who was Scottish born, got into an argument with a pair of English dukes over who invented golf— Scotland or England. The dukes claimed England, James said otherwise. They settled their dispute in a most suitable way: with a game of golf.

Lacking a partner, James called on a fellow named John Patersone, a poor shoemaker who happened to be the best golfer in Edinburgh. James and his golfing ringer whipped the Brits handily, a result largely attributable to Patersone's great abilities. A grateful James not only awarded his partner a sum of money, which Patersone used to build a house, but on Patersone's house the future king placed an escutcheon bearing the emblem of a hand holding a golf club. The escutcheon also bore the words, in Latin, *Far and Sure*, a description of Patersone's golf game that remains, even after all these centuries, as fine a golfing compliment as has ever been uttered.

Golf:
A Game for the
Working Class, Too

Traditionally, golf has been the game of royalty, presidents and prime ministers, power lunchers, and the snooty upper crust. But what is often overlooked is golf's middle-class and working-class origins. The tale of John Patersone and the prince is evidence of that. When the future king went looking for a ringer in his best-ball match with the men from England, he did not turn to the Punch-and-Judy hitters in the royal family; he sought out a tradesman and a member of the so-called lower classes, someone who could really knock the lights out of the ball.

Robert Browning, the golf historian, writes, "Even from the earliest times golf was a game for all classes." In Aulde Scotland *everyone* played: butchers, barkeeps, tailors, coopers, soldiers, ministers, teachers, laborers, field hands, cabinetmakers, along with the lords and ladies. If you did not know the difference between a "spoon" and a "niblick," and know how to use them both, you could hardly lay claim to the title of "Scot."

It was a game of inclusion, not exclusion. A noteworthy golfer, circa 1530, was Sir Robert Maule, described at the time as "ane man of comlie behaviour, of hie stature, sanguine in collure both of hyd and haire, colarique of nature and subject to suddane anger. He had gryt delight in haukine and huntine. Lykewakes he exercisit the gowf, and ofttimes past to Barry Links, quhan the wadsie [bet] was for drink." Tall, handsome, hot-blooded, a hawker, a hunter, a drinker, and a gambler—now that's a golfer for you!

Golf is burdened today by too much respectability, but again, in the days of yore, 'twas not so. In the 1500s, the town elders of St. Andrews, Perth, Leith, and other Scottish burghs slapped stiff fines on golfers for playing on Sundays. People should be in church on the Sabbath, not out on the golf course cursing and gambling and thinking irreligious thoughts about the fellow beating you.

Violence was common on the links. Men argued and fought armed duels. Noses were broken and bloodied and perhaps even snipped off. A Scottish gent once played a game with a monk; the wager was over the monk's nose. If the gent won, the poor monk lost his nose. It's not known whether the monk saved face or not.

In the Edinburgh of 1724, a Captain John Porteous of the local constabulary was one of the top golfers in the city. Being a golfer, however, does not ensure a sterling character. Fact is, golf has as many scoundrels in it as any other game. During a political demonstration on the streets one day, a panicked Porteous fired into the crowd and ordered his men to do the same. The outraged citizenry threw Porteous in jail and eventually strung him up in public view on a city street.

Another less than upstanding swinger of clubs was a gentleman named Halbert Logan, who was in the middle of a game when he received a summons to appear in court over charges that he had participated in a conspiracy against the Scottish king. Logan said this was ridiculous and dismissed the messenger. A little while later the messenger came back and said the court had reconsidered—it was now charging Logan with treason. "Well, well," said Logan, who promptly threw down his clubs, jumped a horse, and escaped to England.

On Being a
Good Golf Companion

Anyone who plays golf will tell you that nothing can spoil a game quicker than a bad partner. "Golf is twenty percent mechanics and technique," wrote Grantland Rice. "The other eighty percent is philosophy, humor, tragedy, romance, melodrama, companionship, camaraderie, cussedness, and conversation." A bad partner is a person who has become obsessed with the 20 percent mechanical side of golf and turned his back on the other, larger part. The pleasures in being outside, the great green natural landscape that surrounds him, the ancient, historical rhythms that underlie his every stroke—these are lost on him in his humorless, ego-driven, club-wielding compulsiveness. A bad partner emits a foul odor, like a skunk; the only solution is to either get rid of the skunk or get away as quickly as you can.

A good golf partner, on the other hand, is one of the blessings of civilization. A good golf partner is someone who will pick up a round of drinks after a round of play. Who will, unless requested otherwise, keep his advice to himself. Who will not crowd you on your tee shot and who doesn't start walking until after you hit. Who does not treat every shot as if he were Nicklaus on the 72nd hole at the Masters. Who knows when to make small talk and when to be serious. Who can tell a good joke ("A man on the tee of the first hole addresses his ball, swings, and whiffs. 'Hmmmn,' he says, 'tough course' ") and who may even know a story about old Arnie Palmer or Lee Trevino that will help fill in the empty spaces of the day.

Who plays golf alone? Once in a while you may, but mostly you do not. You play with your wife, your brother or sister, your father-in-law, your associates at work, your friends, and if none of them is available and you get a good draw at the muni, sometimes you hook up with strangers who, by the end of the day, may be strangers no more. Golf, as has been noted, is a *shared* activity. "Golf camaraderie," writes John Updike, who plays himself, "is based on a common experience of transcendence; fat or thin, scratch or duffer, we have been somewhere together where nongolfers never go."

There's a famous story about Ben Hogan, who was as gifted on a golf course as he was solemn and silent. He played an entire round of eighteen without letting so much as a word issue from his lips until his partner, desperate for some kind of utterance from the great man, asked him to please say something. Hogan looked at him and said, "You're away." All of us, unless we play like Hogan, would do well to stop hitting balls now and then and turn our sights on the other 80 percent of the game, which affords so much of its satisfaction and joy. We should do this for no other reason than to make life nicer for our golf partners.

Caddies, Not Servants

To the nongolfing observer, a man carrying another man's clubs smacks of subservience and class privilege—the country club or even colonialist ethos commonly associated with the game. But the venerable practice of caddying is more complicated than that. Many of the older Scottish courses, which were not designed with condominium living in mind, are nearly impossible for a newcomer to negotiate on his own. A caddie acts as guide. He is also friend, coach, teacher, adviser, referee, links philosopher, wit. A foreign visitor was playing the Old Course at St. Andrews and hacking away horribly. On the 14th, gazing down at the Sahara-like vision of Hell Bunker, he asked his caddie, "Can I carry all that sand?" "I doubt it," said the caddie. "It weighs about twenty-one tons."

The most famous caddie in the world today is a Swedish woman, Fanny Sunesson, who carries for the greatest golfer in the world, Nick Faldo. A famous caddie of another time was Andrew Dickson. As a young boy living in the late 1600s Andrew used to carry the clubs of the duke of York and, as a writer described it, "run before him and announce where the balls fell." Such a pastime for a boy! To race about the open fields, breathing in the fresh sea-laden air, and then, finding a ball in the deep rough, to shout: "Hey Duke, you dweeb! You shanked another one!"

In the days of Andrew Dickson caddies were merely boys, but by the middle of the seventeenth century, a transformation occurred. The caddie became a kind of tradesman, versed in the ways of the golfing tools and knowledgeable in the geography of the links, both spiritual and physical. A caddie was a red-blooded, hard-drinking man of substance who often earned his living at golf and demanded respect from the people he worked for. Caddies carried your bags while on the course, but they did not stoop to do it. Another well-known St. Andrews story is told about a man who forgot his jacket in the clubhouse and asked his caddie to go back and get it. "Go get it yourself," the caddie shot back. "I'm paid to carry—not fetch and carry."

The caddies of long ago were a diverse and colorful lot. "Big" Crawford was a behemoth of a man who used to intimidate players by raising up like a bear and growling at them. He once threw a horseshoe at a player he didn't like, and he referred to Grand Duke Michael of Russia as "Mr. Mike." Caddy Willie (William Gunn was his real name) wore four suits at a time—one on top of the other —as well as three hats sewn together. A colleague, Mad Mac, was a similar dresser, wearing three ties and a long overcoat, even in the heat. He would study a putt through binoculars without glass and advise his boss, "Hit it slightly straight, sir."

Lang Willie, who stood six feet six inches tall, was another prominent member of the species. In St. Andrews, the ecclesiastical home of golf, there is a legend about how when caddies die their spirits mount an invisible ladder into heaven from the first tee. For every lie they've told in life, they must mark each rung on the ladder with chalk. After Lang Willie died, he met one of his counterparts, Donald Blue, coming down the ladder as he was going up.

"Why are you climbing down?" Lang Willie asked.

"I ran out of chalk," Donald Blue said.

Lies? A good caddie tells as many lies as Fagin did. The purpose being to stroke the ego of the man you're carrying for and get a larger tip. No one can be more loyal than a caddie—how about the barefoot one who used to move the ball to a better lie with his toes?—or more quietly subversive. After Sam Snead said some uncomplimentary things about St. Andrews before the 1946 British Open, the caddies tried to sabotage him by incorrectly "clubbing" him. If the shot called for a 7-iron, for instance, the caddie recom-

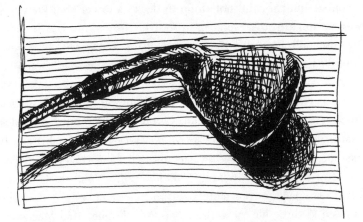

mended a 6. Snead got the last laugh and won the tournament, but he never came back to play the British again.

And if you're speaking of subversion, one cannot overlook Ogden Nash's caddie, who, according to the author, "had chronic hiccups, hay fever, whistled through his teeth, and had large shoes that squeaked."

In the very early days of golf there were no restraining ropes to keep galleries off the fairways. Crowd control was another job left to the caddie. Gradually over the course of a big match in Edinburgh, the people drew in closer and closer until on the 8th green, as the golfer sank a four-foot putt, one of the spectators went to inspect the hole before the golfer himself did. His caddie, at last, had had his fill of it, and grabbed the offender by the scruff of his shirt and jammed his nose into the hole. "Do you see it now?" he demanded. "There's no doubt it's in the hole. But if you still doubt it, wiggle your nose and you'll feel it!"

The best caddie stories show streaks of rebellion, a defiance of authority, and frequently ridicule the man playing golf, i.e., the employer. "What on earth shall I take now?" Harry Vardon asked his caddie after a disappointing shot. "Well, sir, I'd recommend the 4:05 train." A Scottish caddie was working for a man who got so irritated with his poor play that he threw down his clubs and said he was going off to drown himself in the bay. "Go ahead," said the caddie. "You couldn't keep your head down long enough anyway." In the minds of the old-time professional caddies—and most of these fellows, it is true, have climbed the invisible ladder—the whole master-servant thing was reversed. They did all the thinking on the course after all, and the man actually striking the ball was carrying out *their* orders.

In America, the tradition is not as strong as it is in Britain, but there are still plenty of homegrown caddie stories. Porky Oliver's caddie used to keep money in his shoe. You could always tell when Porky was going good because his caddie walked around the course lopsided. Playing late in the day, a man hit a ball that he couldn't find in the hazy afternoon light. "Did that go straight?" he asked. To which the caddie responded: "I couldn't see it, but it sounded crooked." Yet another has Sam Snead facing a long carry over a lake to a green. "How far to the green?" he asks his caddie, who tells him, "Well, yesterday I caddied for Jay Hebert and he hit an eight-iron." After going with the 8 and plopping the ball into the water, Snead is furious. "You mean to tell me Jay Hebert hit an eight-iron from here?" "Yes, sir, he did," says the caddie. "And he hit it into the lake, too."

Many of the game's greatest players started as caddies: Hogan, Palmer, Byron Nelson, Walter Hagen, Seve Ballesteros, to name but a few. Caddies have marched down the course of golfing history. All the great moments in tournament play have been witnessed by caddies, who may have made them possible by advising on the club to be used. The Chicago area, for one, has a thriving caddie program aimed at teaching youngsters the benefits of the game. The pros still use them of course, and if they ever do away with caddies at St. Andrews, they will have to enlist Scotland Yard to find the busloads of Americans and others wandering the heath in search of the next hole.

Even so, it's a dying trade. Caddies are steadily going the way of the village smithy and the barrelmaker, rendered obsolete by changing times and the golf cart. The golf cart is the chief culprit. It carries your clubs just as well and doesn't snicker when you dislodge a robin's nest from a tree with your tee shot. But then again, a golf cart could never produce a line such as heard by Toney Penna, the golf-club designer. After socking a high drive that he lost in the sun, Penna asked his caddie if he knew where his ball went. "I don't know," said the caddie. "I marked it with those birds, but they flew away."

"Fore!"
and Other War Stories

Golf, branded as the game of the effete and the elderly, may boast more war heroes in its honor rolls than any other sport. Freddie Tait, a charismatic Scot who twice won the British Amateur, was killed while leading an attack during the Boer War. Freddie was a good sportsman who would kick an opponent's ball out of a bad lie if the fellow complained about it. Alister Mackenzie, who codesigned Augusta National, served as a surgeon in Africa during the Boer War. John Low, a British Army general in India, was a somewhat more eccentric figure. He used to ride around the golf course on a white horse, dismounting to take his shots. He was in his nineties at the time.

Ernest Jones, one of the game's great early teachers, lost a leg below the knee during World War I. He stayed in the hospital four months. The day after leaving he shot a one-legged round of 83. Despite his handicap Jones was so dexterous with a golf club that he could sit in a chair and drive a ball two hundred yards. Another veteran of World War I was Tommy Armour, who served in the British tank corps and nearly lost his sight in one eye during a battle. Armour went on to win the U.S. Open, the PGA, and the British Open playing with metal plates in his arm and head.

The contribution of golfers in World War II was no less auspicious. Bobby Locke, a master putter who won four British Opens, was a bomber pilot. Bob Sweeny, winner of the 1937 British Amateur who went down to the wire against Arnold Palmer before losing the 1954 U.S. Amateur to him, was a mainstay of the Eagle Squadron, a group of American pilots who flew for the Royal Air Force. Lloyd Mangrum, who shot a 64 in the first round of the 1940 Masters and who was a top money-winner on the tour for years, won two Purple Hearts after being wounded at the Battle of the Bulge. And then there was that high-handicapper, an American chap, who directed the invasion of Normandy and commanded the Allied forces in Europe. Eisenhower, I think the name was.

Besides the men who served in combat, golf has a linguistic connection to war and the military. Some of the most colorful terms in the most colorful of all sporting languages derive from military usage. "Caddie" comes from the French *cadet*, an apprentice in the army. Soldiers under fire seek refuge in bunkers, while golfers launch bombs into them. A bunker is formally defined as a "chest or box," and so it seems to many golfers trying to get out of one. According to the same dictionary, a golfer who "spread-eagles" the other competitors in a tournament has beaten them by a large number of strokes. "Spread-eagling" was a British military term for tying a man up and flogging him.

Even those silly knickers that Payne Stewart sports about in are said to have a military association. In World War I, British officers were instructed to turn the trousers of their uniforms down over their knees "plus four inches." Thus, "plus fours."

When they sound the call of "Fore!" all golfers, ancient and modern, are echoing a sixteenth-century Scottish battle cry. "Ware before!" was a warning to foot soldiers to drop to the ground so that guns might be fired from behind them at an attacking enemy. "Ware before!" gradually evolved into the one-syllable, nearly universal cry of "Fore!" which, like penicillin, was borne of conflict but has saved the lives of people round the globe.

Of Mashies, Niblicks, Mulligans, and Foozlin'

〰️

One can get lost in the language of golf. That's not a 5-iron in your bag; that's a "mashie." The mashie did not get its name because it looked like a potato grinder; it derives from the way people hit the ball when they used it centuries ago: *they mashed it*. A "niblick" is another antiquarian name for a club. It's the equivalent of a 9-iron and probably owes its origin—no one can be sure—to the Scottish word "nib," or short-nose, describing the steep loft of the club. You might have pulled out your trusty niblick if your lie was in the rut of a horse cart.

A "spoon" is obvious—a fairway wood, nowadays the 3-wood, whose curving face resembled the thing you feed babies with. The "brassie" was a wooden club outfitted with a brass plate to give it more punch than an ordinary spoon. None of these clubs should be confused with the "cleek," or 1-iron. Peter Davies, the lexicographer, says that in the nineteenth century "cleek" was also spelled "click," for the sound the club made when striking the ball. By any name, the 1-iron is well nigh impossible to handle. A more modern name for it might be "the damnit," based on the sound a golfer makes after he uses one.

The "baffy" was a wooden club—a 4-wood, in today's lingo. The "sammy" was not named in honor of the late, great Sammy Davis, Jr., the former beringed and bejeweled host of the Greater Hartford Open; it's a term, long gone out of use, for an iron.

As golf changes, so does the language. In the last century they spoke of the "fair green," not the fairway, and you didn't drive the ball off the tee, you "swiped" it. For that matter, there was no such thing as a "tee," those hardworking little wooden pegs we now take for granted. Golfers used to dip into a box of sand located at the start of each hole and hit off tiny mounds of sand they built for themselves.

In more contemporary usage, a "Texas wedge" is a putter played from outside the green, in honor of Ben Hogan and other Texans who used their putters that way. The driver has lots of names: Big Lumber, Big Gun, Big Daddy, Big Dog. The next time you're stepping up to hit, instead of saying, "I think I'll utilize my driver on this hole," you might say, "Let the Big Dog eat." But if you're not careful, the Big Dog will lead you into tiger country or, as it is also referred to, "the asparagus," "the cabbage," "the lettuce," "Marlboro country," "the tall and uncut," or simply, "jail."

Mark Calcavecchia, the free-wheeling American pro who won the 1989 British Open, is a walking golf-slang dictionary. And many of the terms he uses he invents himself. In Calcavecchia-speak, a hook is a "yank," and when you're yanking it too much, you're going to find yourself in the "gunch," or rough. A "power lip," or "bonsai lip," is a putt that knocks against the rim of the hole. A four-putt is a "four jack," a badly hooked ball is a "smother toe," and a birdie (naturally) is a "tweeter."

The aviary of golf is well stocked. The "eagle" and "birdie" have prominent places, but the "albatross" (double eagle) and "buzzard" (double bogey) are not used much in this country. The "duck hook," you should know, has nothing to do with birdlife; it describes the dipping action of the ball after it's hit.

Golf is a frustrating game. There can be no clearer testimony to this fact than the number of terms in a golfer's vocabulary that describe failure. Scuff, smother, stub, hook, snap hook, slice, muff, duff, flub, fluff, hitting too fat or too thin, hack, skull, spray, scuffle, socketing, top, baff, chop, twitch, yip, shank, dub, banana ball. Some of these terms are ancient and out-of-date; some are still in vogue. But they all describe a form of mishit. And there are plenty more. One who "foozles"—that is, muffs a shot—on a consistent basis might be described as a foozler, though not to his face. It is true that foozlers have been known to sclaff. A "sclaff" is a little like "chili-dipping," only not as easy to picture. They think "chili-dipping" comes from dipping a chip into hot sauce, which resembles a golf club digging up some turf before it hits the ball. (The Tex-Mex influence is present, too, in "margarita," a putt that goes around the cup in a circle but doesn't go in.) "Miss the globe" is an obsolete phrase for a silent shot, an aerial swat, an air shot, a whiff—in short, utter humiliation. And on and on. As long as we keep finding new ways to butcher a golf ball, we will invent new ways to describe it.

Ah, but there's hope. That's the genius of the "mulligan." When Pandora opened her box, allowing Envy, Greed, Dishonesty, and other evils to escape, she also let out Hope. Hope, for golfers, is the mulligan. It is the tee ball that never happened. Erase the tape and start over. Nobody can say how the term came about or if there actually was a Mr.—or Mrs. or Miss—Mulligan. But golfers owe old Mulligan an incalculable debt. For where else in this life does one get a chance to wipe the slate clean and act as if nothing at all went wrong?

Some Thoughts
on How Many Clubs to Carry

Golf rules stipulate that a player can carry no more than fourteen clubs in his bag. The reasoning behind this is to prevent such abuses as those of Light Horse Harry Cooper, who carried twenty-six clubs at a time, and Lawson Little, who toted thirty. Bobby Jones carried twenty-two clubs in his 1920 U.S. Amateur championship final. Other golfers, while not going in for such quantity, have carried specialized clubs. Leo Diegel packed four drivers (one for a hook, one for a slice, and two for varying wind conditions), while Chick Evans matched him with four putters.

Turn-of-the-century golfers would have thought all this special-ization silly and unnecessary, as they carried only eight or so clubs and got along just fine. Some analysts, harkening back to this simpler, less cluttered time, have argued that the nineties trend toward greater and greater specialization in playing clubs is a doleful one for the game, for it implies that every different situation demands a different type of club. Good golf, they say, is an expression of resourcefulness and ingenuity; and being creative in the use of your clubs is one of the most appealing and fundamentally satisfying parts of the game.

However you line up in the argument, a good rule of thumb might be to carry one or two spares in your bag in case you get upset at your driver or putter and decide to wrap one of them around a tree. You're also going to have to face the possibility that no matter how many or what type of clubs you have, none is going to live up to the high expectations you have set for it. You may then feel much the same as that old English lord who, after four-putting a green, instructed his caddie, "Pick up the ball, have the clubs destroyed, and leave the course."

Fathers, Sons, Mothers, and Daughters

✐

Golf is not only a game of fathers and sons. It is a game of fathers, sons, mothers, and daughters. The history of golf extends for hundreds of years, but the past is wedded to the present by the simple, ever-lasting act of a parent giving his son or daughter some clubs to play with, like a family heirloom passed from one generation to the next. Nancy Lopez got her chance when she was eight years old. Her father, Domingo, was an excellent golfer, and Nancy used to trail her father and mother around when they played at the municipal course in Roswell, New Mexico, where they lived. Then her moment came. Domingo handed his daughter a 4-wood and said to her, "Hit it. You just keep hitting it until you get that ball in the hole." Her dad became her coach, and she has relied on him for advice and instruction throughout her career.

King James of Britain, who ruled in the early 1600s, was an avid golfer who taught his sons the game. From King James to Domingo Lopez—that's a thumbnail sketch of the evolution of golf, and a blueprint for the future. Each link in the chain consists of a father's outstretched hand, clasped to his son's or daughter's. But let's not forget Mom. In golf, she's in there, too. The sixteen-year-old Greg Norman, growing up in Queensland, Australia, caddied for his mother. After she finished playing she'd let him have a go at it. Ben Crenshaw's first golf clubs were a set of Patty Bergs that belonged to his mother.

The single most evocative image in golf in recent memory is that of a parent, Jack Nicklaus, hugging his son, Jack Jr., on the 72nd green after the father's emotional win at the 1986 Masters. Jack Jr. served as caddie, too. Nicklaus was himself influenced by the death of his father at a critical time in his career. After extraordinary early success he went into a slump at the end of the sixties. His father contracted cancer in the fall of 1969 and died the following year. The son felt the loss deeply. "He felt as though he had let his dad down in the last years of his life," said Barbara Nicklaus, explaining her husband's state of mind. But Nicklaus came back to the game with renewed determination, played himself out of his funk, and won the 1970 British Open.

After Johnny Miller's brother died in a fishing accident, his father took him to the San Francisco Golf Club to give him formal lessons for the first time. Johnny was seven. His dad thought it would be a way to get his mind off the accident. Up until then Johnny had worked on his golf game at home, hitting balls into a net rigged up by his father in their basement.

Colman McCarthy, the writer, believes that you can't force an interest in golf. "Children cannot be taught golf," he says. "They can only be exposed to it." McCarthy, who played competitive golf in college, writes how he would go out to the course with his wife and sons—ages eight, seven, and four. While Mom and Dad negotiated the fairways and greens in the customary manner, the boys played in their own way, running through sand traps, climbing trees, sliding down hills. Gradually, they came to want to try their hand with the clubs and hit shots.

When Sandy Lyle was a baby, his parents set him on a blanket in the rough along the 18th fairway at the course in Scotland where they worked. His father, Alex, was the head pro, and his mother helped run the pro shop. While Agnes worked inside, she kept an eye on little Sandy from a window in the shop. Sandy got his first golf club from his parents at the age of three. At an older age he won the Masters and the British Open.

Peter Robertson was a countryman of Lyle's, though from a much earlier time. He lived in St. Andrews and died in 1803. That was when a golf ball was made of feathers stuffed inside a leather jacket. Ballmaking was Peter Robertson's trade, and his son, David, followed in his father's footsteps and became a respected golf player, teacher, and caddie. And in turn his son, Allan Robertson—grandson of Peter—reached the top of the ladder. Allan was the best player in Britain in the middle 1800s, which is as good as saying he was the best player in the world. Considered an innovator in his use of the irons, Allan was the first truly professional golfer, a man who played matches for money. It was said that he never beat an opponent so badly that they could raise the stakes against him for the next match. He kept things close and competitive, the money flowing—yet he always won.

Sandy Lyle, in swaddling clothes along the 18th fairway at Hawkstone Park. Allan Robertson, whose toys as a child were golf clubs. Jump forward, jump back. Golf is not a linear progression; it's a circle. Let the circle be unbroken.

Tom Morris tutored under Allan Robertson, and after his mentor passed from the scene, Morris became the best in the land. But Old Tom, as he was called, was surpassed as a golfer by his son, Young Tom, who, sadly, never got the chance to be old. Young Tom died at age twenty-four on Christmas Day—heartbroken, it was said, over the death of his wife in childbirth earlier in the year. But in his short time at the game Young Tom towered over his contemporaries, winning the 1869 and 1870 British Opens—then a 36-hole event— by eleven and twelve strokes, respectively. In 1869, Old Tom finished second to his son.

Old Tom, Young Tom. Davis Love II and III. Jack Burke, Sr., Jack Burke, Jr. Burke senior tied for second in the 1920 U.S. Open; Burke junior won both the Masters and the PGA in 1956. The runner- up in that year's Masters was Ken Venturi, who learned his golf at Harding Municipal Park in San Francisco where his dad ran the pro shop. While his dad worked, Ken practiced and played, and as a precocious teenager he began competing in national junior tourna- ments. He won the U.S. Open and was twice runner-up at the Masters, losing the second time to another man with golf in his genes, Arnold Palmer.

As a member of its construction crew, Arnold's father, Deacon Palmer, helped build Latrobe Country Club in Pennsylvania. In 1921, when it opened, he joined the greenskeeping staff. Over the years he became head greenskeeper, teaching pro, and finally, superinten- dent. In the meantime, his son learned to play a little golf. And when Arnold got to be rich and famous, he bought Latrobe Country Club.

Young Arnold started playing when he was four; Deacon cut some clubs down to size for him. It was the same with Tony Jacklin. Jacklin's father took up golf late in life and his son caddied for him. After Dad was done, the future British Open champion and Ryder Cup captain would take his cuts with a lady's chopped-down 3-wood. Bruce Devlin got serious about the game after his father suffered a horrible car accident that severed his arm from his body. Devlin's father continued to play with one arm and actually shaved six strokes off a twenty handicap. He was nonetheless sensitive about his condition and would not play with anyone but his son. His son was eager to please. "I sensed that if I played well, it would lift him out of his depression," recalled Bruce years later.

It's a happy fact that, in golf, a woman can take up the calling as well as a man and go on to achieve great things. And even if she does not surpass her father in the game, she can still advise him on it. Playing on the Senior Tour, Orville was as Moody as his name until his daughter Michelle became his caddy. "You've got a crappy attitude," she told him at one point, and the blunt message helped shape up his disposition and his game. In 1983, George Archer became the first golfer to use a female caddie at the tradition-bound Masters. The caddie was his daughter, Jill. Furious with himself for playing a poor round, Archer received unusual support from his caddie: "I still love you, Daddy," Jill told him, and leaned over and kissed him.

Asked how he would like to be remembered, Ray Floyd said, "I would like some father to be able to say to his son, 'Watch Ray Floyd play golf. He conducts himself in the proper manner. He doesn't throw clubs; he doesn't have tantrums; he is a gentleman.' " Fathers want to give to sons, and sons want to give back to fathers. That's the way it's supposed to work, and if you're lucky, that's the way it does. Scott Simpson, a U.S. Open winner, received his first golf clubs when he was ten. His dad divvied up a set of his clubs, giving his brother David the odds and Scott the evens. In appreciation Scott caddied for his father when he played in a recent Senior Open. More moving was Curtis Strange's tribute to his father after Strange's first U.S. Open win. Strange's father died when he was fourteen. "From age nine everything my father taught me about the golf swing is still with me," Strange said in the interview room after his hard-fought 18-hole playoff victory. And then Curtis began to cry. "This," he said, "is for my dad."

Golf in the New World

One of the earliest mentions we have of golf in America dates from 1650, when a ne'er-do-well named Jacob Jansz attacked a tavern-keeper and another fellow with a golf club and was tossed in jail for it. This, according to the minutes of the upstate New York Dutch colony where Jansz lived and functioned as a one-man crime wave. On June 2, 1649, Jansz threw a tankard, "without cause," in the face of a court messenger, for which he was fined. (Presumably the tankard was empty, Jansz having drained its contents into his belly.) Two months later an unrepentant Jansz was in trouble with the law again, knocking one Willem Jeuriaensz flat onto his back and coldcocking another guy who was coming to Willem's aid. The next year Jansz got into a brawl with three other people, all of whom suffered injuries inflicted by our hero. You'd think that the good folks of Jansz's hometown would begin to catch on to him, but no, here he is again, on December 12, 1650, taking out his liquor-fueled frustrations on another unfortunate barkeep. But this time his weapon of choice was not a beer mug, but "a golf club," as the court minutes clearly state. The court minutes do not, however, specify what club Jansz was wielding—driver? spoon? mashie?—so this must remain a matter of historical speculation.

The earliest reference to a person or persons actually *playing* golf—whacking someone over the head with a 3-wood is not, in all good conscience, consistent with the finest traditions of the game—is contained in a 1659 ordinance from Fort Orange, a Dutch colony that later became Albany, New York. In the spirit of King James II, who banned golf in Scotland two centuries earlier for reasons of national defense, the town fathers of Fort Orange outlawed golf in the name of public safety. The ordinance, which appears to be aimed at curbing the tendencies of wild hitters off the tee, reads thusly: "Having heard divers complaints from the burghers of this place against the practice of playing golf along the streets, which causes great damage to the windows of the houses, and also exposes people to being injured . . . [the magistrates] hereby forbid all persons to play golf in the streets." If they disobeyed and played anyway, they would be fined.

Now it may be that both of these early references are not to the game we know, but rather to an old Dutch game called *kolven*, which some historians think was a sporting ancestor to golf, much as cricket is to baseball. Historical quibbles aside, there can be no doubt that Scottish soldiers stationed in New York at the time of the Revolutionary War were playing real golf, a primitive but recognizable brand of the game we play today. The *Royal Gazette* of April 21, 1779, published by the printer James Rivington, carried this advertisement:

To the GOLF PLAYERS

The Season for this pleasant and healthy Exercise now advancing, Gentlemen may be furnished with excellent CLUBS and the veritable Caledonian BALLS, by enquiring at the Printer's.

Besides being a printer, Rivington was a shopkeeper who sold golf clubs and those state-of-the-art feather-stuffed Caledonians. This may be our earliest record of a preseason golf sale, an eighteenth-century version of a Nevada Bob's or Las Vegas Discount.

Golf—again, the real thing—was played in South Carolina even before the Revolutionary War. Andrew Johnson, a Charleston merchant, returned home after a business trip to Scotland with some golf clubs or, as they were referred to in those days, "goof sticks." Johnson may or may not have been a member of the South Carolina Golf Club, whose pioneering members enjoyed their favorite pastime on Harleston Green, a public park in Charleston. Savannah, Georgia, was the home of another pre–Revolutionary War club; they also used a public park as the site of their play.

Although played in pockets of the South and the North in the 1700s and early 1800s, golf did not really catch on and take root in America until that famous Yonkers gang came onto the scene in 1888. For golfers, 1888 is like 1066 to English schoolchildren or 1776 for Americans—it's a date you must know, or you can hardly call yourself educated in a links way. The story begins with Robert Lockhart, a Yonkers businessman, making a trip to Scotland and returning with some golf equipment, much as Andrew Johnson had done a century before. Lockhart carried in his possession a driver, a brassie (2-wood), a spoon (3-wood), a cleek (long iron), another iron, a putter, and two dozen gutta-percha balls. The clubs were made by none other than golf's Father Time himself, Old Tom Morris.

Jazzed by his new playthings, Lockhart and his sons went out to Riverside Drive in New York City to give them a whirl. One story says that Lockhart was such a crazy hitter, and his new activity so utterly strange to the citizens of the metropolis, that one of New York's Finest came by and arrested him. In fact, a New York City cop happening by on horseback was so intrigued by what Lockhart was doing—or attempting to do—that he asked if he could try, too. The officer dismounted and, according to an account by Lockhart's son Sydney, unleashed a beauty of a drive on his first attempt. Flushed by his success, the cop decided to get ambitious and really sock one—a deadly sin, as every golfer knows. Here, let's turn the narrative over to Sydney Lockhart (as told to H. B. Martin): "Being greatly encouraged and proud of his natural ability at a game that involved a ball and stick, he tried again. This time he missed the ball completely, and then in rapid succession he missed the little globe three more times; so with a look of disgust on his face he mounted his horse and rode away."

Robert Lockhart may have had a golf experience similar to the policeman's, for soon after his outing on Riverside Drive he turned his Morris-mades over to his pal John Reid and dropped forever from the pages of golf history. No matter. He left his sticks in good hands. Seizing an opportunity for some real fun, Reid gathered five of his friends together, ventured out to a cow pasture in Yonkers, and knocked those gutta-perchas around like nobody's business. It being winter in New York, snow and bad weather quickly put their game on hiatus. But they were back at it the following spring and summer. After a game in the late fall the group adjourned to Reid's house and over dinner and drinks, officially began the St. Andrew's Golf Club (like the Scottish St. Andrews only with an apostrophe), which still exists today. The St. Andrew's club was a leader in the early years of the game here, and its establishment—November 14, 1888—is considered a benchmark. The Scottish pastime had come to the United States to stay, and in the next century the numbers of Americans taking up the game, and the high level of skill the best ones showed, would transform and vitalize the ancient game.

Democracy and the Golf Ball

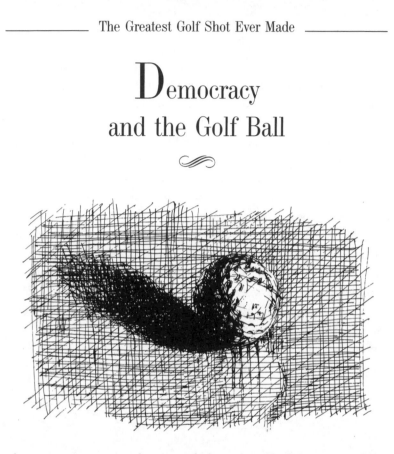

The American energy that surged through golf at the onset of the new century changed the game from the ground up, starting with its most fundamental object. An otherwise obscure Cleveland business-man named Coburn Haskell invented a new kind of golf ball that came onto the market in the early 1900s. This revolutionary creation, a ball with a rubber center, would have a greater impact on the game than anything Bobby Jones or Arnold Palmer or even Deane Beman ever did.

Coburn Haskell was to golf what Henry Ford was to cars, or Steven Jobs to computers. He put it within reach of the ordinary person.

The "featherie," or feather-stuffed ball, dates back to the days of golfing antiquity. The early featheries were stuffed with cow's hair, wool, or fine-grained wood. From the 1600s on, they consisted of feathers packed into a leather cover. Featheries were just like any other golf ball; how far they traveled depended on who was hitting them. A good player routinely sent his featherie two hundred yards; if he really popped it, it would go much farther. The English kings employed men who made featheries for them, but the job was hard and the bennies were few. "The employment is accounted unhealthy," reads an 1823 account, "and many of the ball-makers have been observed to fall sacrifice to consumption." The hard physical labor of stuffing and stitching that small leather package, while breathing in feathers all day, did not tend to increase the life expectancy of your average nine-to-five ballmaker.

The arrival of the gutta-percha ball in the middle 1800s was a welcome development for golfers, as well as those ballmakers who were around to see it. The guts of a "guttie," as it was called, came from the sap of a Malaysian family of trees. Stories of how it was discovered differ, but no one disputes its wide and pervasive impact. It was cheaper and more easily produced than the old featherie, and from a purely golfing standpoint, it was much the superior ball. People such as Allan Robertson and Young Tom Morris could make the guttie dance and spin as if it were attached to a string. In their hands guttie golf was a thing of ball-manipulating beauty, demanding great craft and skill, as Ben Crenshaw and Jack Nicklaus found out when they conducted an experiment with one a few years ago at St. Andrews. Masters winner Crenshaw went first and hit his specially made guttie two hundred yards on the fly. Nicklaus was not so fortunate. He chili-dipped his first swing and the ball dribbled along the ground for only fifteen or twenty yards. Nicklaus changed clubs on his next attempt, but that old guttie, which apparently had not been informed of the great man's reputation, still went nowhere. "There's something wrong with this ball," said the puzzled Nicklaus.

While it had many good qualities, the guttie could not compete with the rubber-cored ball when it was introduced by Haskell and an associate with the Goodrich Rubber Company. Predictably, the guttie had its loyalists, but after Sandy Herd won the 1902 British Open using Haskell's ball, it was just a matter of time before the guttie joined the featherie in the golf-ball graveyard. The new rubber core flew higher and rolled farther, and its coming led to a change in the type of sticks golfers used. The old hickory clubs couldn't take the punishment dished out by the Haskell ball, and steel-shafted clubs came into being in the thirties. Dimples and a few other wrinkles were added to improve the Haskell ball in its early years, but its basic concept—wound elastic threads around a rubber center—is identical to the Titleists and Maxflis of today. The Haskell patent expired in 1915, and other U.S. companies, seeing a new market opening up, jumped into the business of providing golf balls for the millions of people now taking up this suddenly less exclusive game.

The Universality of Dufferdom

One is struck by how little golf has changed over the years. Over the centuries, even. The composition of the ball has changed, but it remains a stubborn little object that insists on doing what it wants to do and not what you want it to. We don't play with hickory- or wood-shafted clubs anymore. But the function of a golf club is no different today than it was for those ancient Scottish sheeptenders who, according to legend, invented golf by hitting rocks into holes with sticks. All a golf club is—make no mistake about it—is a highly sophisticated stick. (Remember that the next time you lay down four hundred clams for that new Mizuno driver with the steel head and low-torque, graphite-boron shaft.) It's the same thing with these multimillion-dollar designer courses cropping up all over Hawaii and places like that. Gussy it up as you will, golf is still basically a target game played on an improved cow pasture.

Another common ingredient of the game is what might be called the universality of dufferdom. The Faldos and Nicklauses come and go, but we duffers are the real backbone of the game. It may be the case that the truly terrible golfers love the game more than the exceptional ones, for they stick with it through thick and (mostly) thin; though the duffed shots overrun the good; though the double and triple and quadruple bogeys far outnumber the pars or—a consummation devoutly to be sought!—the birdies. We duffers do not need to achieve perfection or anything close to it to love golf; just throw us a bone once in a while—a well-struck 3-wood or a chip from the frog hairs that rolls to within inches of the can—and we're happy.

The word "sclaff" has gone out of use, but who does not know what Mr. Dalrymple, the author of *The Handbook to Golf*, published in 1895, was referring to when he described "the innate malignant tendency to duff and muff and sclaff and miss, and top and heel and toe." Or E. M. Griffith, circa 1909: "Duffed the approach! Oh dash it! What's that? Thirteen . . ." The language may be foreign to the modern ear, but not the sentiment. O brother duffers!

Bobby Jones said that he learned nothing from a successful shot—but that a miscue gave him a chance to learn something that would improve his game. If that's the case, then duffers are the most knowledgeable of all golfers, for they have so many more opportunities for continuing education.

It's ironic that some of the world's most powerful people play golf. For no game is as great a leveler as golf. It costs a great deal of money to play, and many of our leading country clubs have admission policies toward blacks and minorities that would be backward for the twelfth century. But once you get inside the walls, the game itself is a spirited and remarkably egalitarian exercise. Do we think that George Bush keeps the ball in the fairway all the time? Hardly. Nor does dufferdom restrict itself to the Republicans. "If I swung the gavel the way I swung that golf club, the nation would be in a helluva mess," said Tip O'Neill when he was Speaker of the House of Representatives. Tip made the remark just after hitting an approach shot into a lake at a pro-am. See, the ball plays no favorites! It knows no distinctions, cares not a whit about the size of your bank account or the cut of your clothes. It metes out equal justice, punishing all.

"Playing the game I have learned the meaning of humility," said Abba Eban, the former foreign minister of Israel. "It has given me an understanding of the futility of human effort." This is one of the perverse appeals of the sport; it cuts us all down to size, no matter how high and mighty we think we are. "It acts as a corrective against sinful pride," wrote P. G. Wodehouse, the British humorist. "I attribute the insane arrogance of the later Roman emperors almost entirely to the fact that, never having played golf, they never knew that strange chastening humility which is engendered by a topped chip shot. If Cleopatra had been ousted in the first round of the Ladies' Singles, we should have heard a lot less of her proud imperiousness."

We are all duffers under the sun. Inside every great or powerful person beats the heart of a duffer. Andrew Carnegie, the industrialist, was one of the wealthiest men of his time, yet an exceedingly average golfer. After selling the Carnegie Corporation to U.S. Steel for the tidy sum of $250 million (and this was in 1901), he went out to the links and got a par on a hole that he had never played well before. Later that day, when he showed up at J. P. Morgan's office in New York to finalize the deal, a friend came up to him and said, "I've been hearing great things about you," referring of course to the sale of his company for a huge profit. But Carnegie looked at the man with utter astonishment and said, "How did you know I had a par on the fifth today?"

Now that's a duffer for you, a man who can think of nothing else but the par he scored that day. Throw in a boast or two about it and you've got the species down to a tee.

A Great American Success Story

Although the British may be sick of it by now, no story in all of golf has such enduring appeal as the story of Francis Ouimet. Ouimet, as many a golfer knows, was the skinny twenty-year-old Massachusetts kid who beat the Englishmen Vardon and Ray to win the 1913 U.S. Open and usher in a new era in the history of golf. Vardon and Ray were then the world's greatest golfers, and England was the dominant golfing nation. Ouimet's shocking upset was like Buster Douglas flooring Mike Tyson or Team USA defeating the Russians in ice hockey in the 1980 Olympics. A heavy underdog had beaten the bullies from overseas and in so doing, turned the sporting world on its head.

The tale of Francis Ouimet is such an appealing one not only because of its historic implications, but because of the central character of Francis himself. He is a genuine American hero. The only reason he may not be better known among the public at large is the misguided perception that golf is a sissy sport and the people who play it wimps. But Francis was everything we Americans look for in a hero, and even fans of baseball, football, basketball, et al.—the so-called "real" sports—may profit from his example.

Every great American story—sports or otherwise—is an immigrant story, and so was Francis's. The Ouimet family (pronounced "we-met") were of French Canadian stock and moved from Quebec to the Boston area when Francis was a boy. Today "Francis" has fallen out of favor as a boy's name, but in a curious way, it may contribute to the Ouimet legend. Would we care as much if his name were Jack or Buck or Rambo Ouimet? Perhaps, perhaps not. But the antiquated, even girlish-sounding name of Francis Ouimet adds to our picture of a shy, awkward, vulnerable youth who, though not old enough to take a legal drink, whipped the powerful Brits at the their own game.

When the Ouimets came to America, they moved into a small house in Brookline across the street from a prestigious New England golf club with the imposing title of The Country Club. (Seventy-five years later a visiting golf pro, Peter Jacobsen, would ask, "The Country Club? Couldn't anybody think of a name for this place?") The Ouimets were hardly country-club material. The closest Francis got to the club was crossing the links in the morning on his way to school. Later he became a caddie and would sneak onto the grounds of the course and play a fast few holes before the greenskeeper showed up for work. When Francis first got hooked on golf, he and his brother Wilfred—now, there's another name for you—rigged up a home-made 3-hole course in the field behind their house. It included a creek, a gravel pit, and grass tall enough to lose a small child in, and Francis negotiated these hazards using hand-me-down clubs and banged-up old balls. But when Ouimet graduated from his homemade course, he took his game—not to the uppity, rarified airs of The Country Club—but to the nearby Franklin Park public course. The man who revolutionized golf in America perfected his game on a public course.

Ouimet's U.S. Open win at, fittingly, The Country Club, "began the transformation of golf in America from an elite game to a public pastime," writes Jaime Diaz. But this champion of the Common Man (and Woman) had to be talked into entering—all he wanted to do was watch the great English champions play, not play against them.

Harry Vardon, a pinpoint-shot artist, and Ted Ray, a burly, heavyset man who was considered the longest driver in the world, were on a newspaper-sponsored exhibition tour of the U.S., and either of them was considered a cinch to win the event. Though he had had some success in tournaments, Ouimet had also experienced considerable failure, and he was not even a long shot in the handicapping prior to the Open. No big reputation followed him into the Open—no reputation of any kind, as a matter of fact. He was a nobody, an extra player they had picked up to fill out the amateur bracket in the field.

Ah, yes. Now there is another reason why Ouimet, though long dead, remains such a vital figure and exerts such a powerful hold on our imaginations. He was an amateur. Not that we have anything against making a buck—more power to you, fella. But a professional is someone who plays for money as well as the love of the game; an amateur—unless he is up to his ears in under-the-table payments, as most of them are—plays simply for the love of it. Ouimet stayed an amateur his entire golf-playing life, though he could most certainly have made money as a professional following his epic, highly publicized triumph.

Ouimet had all the things we require of our heroes, and yet we also recognize that an athlete, in order to be successful, must be supremely confident, if not arrogant, while on the field. Ouimet met this requirement as well as he met all the others, playing with coolness and calm despite adverse circumstances (it rained the final day of the Open and the day of the playoff) and facing such formidable opponents.

Another necessary element to a hero's story is a great comeback, and Ouimet provided that, too. Needing to play the final six holes in two under to tie, Francis picked up his first birdie on 13, on a chip from beyond the green. He came to 17, though, still needing a stroke, and here was where that confidence—the unteachable, un-yielding resolve of a young man who doesn't know that he shouldn't be doing what he is doing—came fully into play. On the green anywhere from ten to twenty feet from the hole—historical accounts, as they so often do, differ—with a tricky downhill roll, Francis did not hesitate. "I have never seen such a putt more confidently played," recalled Ted Ray. "Coming at such a crisis with so much depending on it, I count that stroke as one of the master strokes of golf."

Ouimet's birdie—and par on the next hole—gave him a tie with the two Britishers, and the next day, amid more rain, they played again. The playoff was the Ouimet story in its purest form, boiled down to essences: the Englishmen—not just one, but *both* of them —up against the lone American underdog challenger. Even at this juncture nobody gave Ouimet a chance. But first Ray bowed to the pressure of an 18-hole playoff, then Vardon. "The play was so good, the strain so great, that someone was almost bound to bend under it," noted Bernard Darwin, who was an eyewitness along with many of Ouimet's cheering hometown friends. On the 16th hole, with his game in ruins, the great Vardon lit a cigarette for himself, something that no one could recall ever seeing him do on a golf course.

But Francis did not crack. Heroes never do. He even had the presence of mind to advise a spectator on the 10th tee who asked him how to cure a chronic slice of his.

Ouimet's caddy was named Eddie Lowery, and Eddie may even be a more appealing figure than Francis. Every hero needs a sidekick, right? Don Quixote and Sancho Panza, Huck and Jim, Butch Cassidy and Sundance. Well, Francis had Eddie, who was ten years old and playing hooky from school. Eddie was the perfect partner for Francis. Francis was lanky and thin, Eddie was a pip-squeak. Francis had a long, rubbery face; Eddie wore a serious, nearly dour expression. Both wore ties. Little Eddie's shirtsleeves were rolled up, as if to convey an impression of getting down to business, but wreaking havoc with this image was his sailor's hat with the red band and the brim turned down. Eddie and Francis—what a team! And whenever Francis got discouraged, there was little Eddie to pep him up with his mantralike instructions: "Take your time," Eddie said. "You've got all day." Eddie repeated it to Francis before every shot. "Take your time. You've got all day."

Ouimet's improbable achievement resounds to this day. It was not the first win by an American at the Open—Johnny McDermott of Philadelphia had won it the two previous years—but it was the first against a truly international field, and it helped transform the National Open into a golfing match of significance. The world was, of course, a far different place in 1913. The First World War was still a year away, and the great European monarchies looked as indestructible as ever. At the time America was a minor player on the world scene, and Ouimet's audacious win—especially at the expense of two representatives of the great nineteenth-century colonial power, Britain—might be seen as a symbol of the rise of the twentieth century's newest power, the United States. On a more concrete, less grandiose scale perhaps, Ouimet gave an incalculable boost to golf in America. As news of his feat spread, it inspired others to give the game a try, and golf grew by leaps and bounds in the coming years. And in this, Francis fulfilled the final, and most important, obligation of the hero: his victory was not a victory for himself alone, but for all the others who would follow in his footsteps.

More Immigrant Stories

Francis Ouimet, the first American golf hero, was a Canadian immigrant. Willie Anderson was born on the southeastern coast of Scotland. His family immigrated here in 1895, and six years later

Willie won the first of four U.S. Opens. The adjective most frequently applied to Willie is "dour," but the little sourpuss sure could play. Gene Sarazen was working on his sand game one day, admiring how well he was hitting out of the trap. He was practicing with a compatriot of Anderson's, a former pro, and Sarazen asked him if old Willie could have gotten out of the bunkers as well. "Get out of the bunkers?" said the pro. "Why, he never got in them!"

Sarazen (birth name: Eugenio Saraceni) was himself the son of immigrants and the hero of the many Italian Americans who came to the U.S. in the great wave of migration in the early part of the twentieth century. But for obvious reasons, most of the golf-playing immigrants came from Great Britain, notably Scotland. John Reid, who organized that famous 1888 Yonkers cow-pasture game that led to the permanent establishment of golf in America, was a transplanted Scot. So were the Smith brothers—of golfing, not cough-drop, fame. Macdonald Smith was a great stylist and putter. In this day of the six-hour round his immortal advice, "Miss 'em quick," ought to be stitched into the waistbands of Sansabelts everywhere. His brother Alex won two U.S. Opens but may be better known as the tutor of Glenna Collett Vare, the best American woman golfer of the twenties.

Donald Ross, a native of Dornoch, Scotland, arrived in Boston in 1918 with less than five dollars in his pocket. In time he went south to Pinehurst, North Carolina, where his most sublime creation, Pinehurst No. 2, stands as one of the world's great golf courses. Robert Trent Jones, another noteworthy golf architect, came here from England in 1911. As with Ross and most every other golf-course designer who's ever lived (please see Dye, Pete or Nicklaus, Jack), Jones's creations have often drawn fire when they were first unveiled. But he achieved a measure of revenge against his critics after he revamped the Lower Course at the Baltusrol Golf Club in Springfield, New Jersey. A few of Baltusrol's members had attacked his layout of the 4th hole, an 183-yard par 3 that must carry over a pond, as being too tough. Challenged to play the hole himself, Jones teed up the ball, selected a long iron, and with the members looking on, promptly hit a hole in one.

"I don't agree with you," Jones told them, and walked off.

Jones, Ross, and the other immigrants who came to this country did so for all the traditional reasons: greater opportunity, wider personal freedom, and God bless 'em, a chance to make a buck. And in so doing, they added spice and flavor to what had become a stodgy upper-class game. Walter Travis, an Australian by birth, moved here as a kid. Though he didn't take up the game until his midthirties, his putting was considered especially good. In 1904, playing in the British Amateur, he shook up the golf world with his use of the center-shafted Schenectady putter. The British reacted to Walter's new-styled putter the way today's golfing pooh-bahs regard Karsten Solheim and banned it from their country. (The U.S. allowed it.) Jim Barnes, a native Englishman, came to this country in 1906 and won all the major tournaments of his day. Barnes would look for lucky four-leaf clovers while out on the golf course. If he found one, he kept it in his mouth for the rest of the round. Light Horse Harry Cooper's father was a golf pro who moved the family from England to Texas in search of a better life. His son led all the pros in 1937 with $14,000 in winnings—not bad money for the Depression.

Another foreign-born transplant who made his stake in the U.S.—and certainly added spice to the game in the meantime—was Scotland's Tommy Armour. Armour was an influential golf teacher and writer who also won three majors. He was a small man, but his hands were so large that a sportswriter likened them to "two stalks of bananas." Like so many of the immigrant golfers, Armour earned his bread and butter as a club pro, working for many years at Medinah Country Club outside Chicago. A World War I vet who had suffered head and eye injuries in a tank battle, he was no lapdog for Medinah's members. While he gave lessons, it was a familiar pastime of his to amuse himself by firing at chipmunks on the practice range with a .22-caliber rifle. One day one of his pupils grew impatient with this and demanded, "When are you going to quit that and take care of me?" Armour swung the rifle around toward the complainer and growled, "Don't tempt me."

"Pull the Pin, Eddie" (Walter Hagen—Part I)

In a nearly twenty-year period beginning in 1914, Walter Hagen won a pair of U.S. Opens, four British Opens, the Canadian and French Opens, and five PGA titles, four of them in a row. But to describe Hagen merely as "a golfer" is like saying Einstein was a scientist or Babe Ruth a baseball player. Hagen was a golfer—and so very very much more.

If you need a time period to fix him in, it's the Roaring Twenties. That is indeed apt. Hagen, like Ruth (his drinking and carousing pal), belongs in that roller coaster of an era, a time of speakeasies, stock market speculators, the Charleston, Al Jolson (another Hagen chum) on Broadway, mobsters, prohibitionists, Gatsbyesque dreams, political upheaval, and Clara Bow on the silver screen. "Into this gaudy period," wrote Charles Price, who knew the man, "stepped the Haig, as he was called, with the sangfroid of a Valentino, his black hair pomaded to an iridescence, his handsome features browned by the sun and the wind until they had the hue of brierwood." You like cool? Let's talk Walter.

Hagen's philosophy of golf was: "Never hurry and don't worry." Walter seldom worried about anything, least of all money, and he never hurried even though he once kept a president of the United States, Warren Harding, cooling his heels on the first tee while he finished shaving. On a tour of the Far East at the height of his fame, Hagen showed up two hours late for a match with a Japanese prince. Informed that you just didn't keep a member of the royal family waiting like that, Hagen said, "Well, he wasn't going anywhere, was he?" Haig and the prince played their delayed round of golf, and the prince was as charmed by his partner as everyone else was.

Another of Hagen's famous sayings—"You're here only for a short visit, so never forget to stop and smell the flowers"—is a nearly perfect capsule description of his own life. Hagen, a Rochester, New York native who never graduated from the eighth grade, smelled so many flowers in his life his nose must've hurt. He loved champagne and fine food and clothes. He made a million bucks and, it's said, spent a million. He loved going out on the town and living it up with the rich and famous people who sought out his company. One of his favorite golf pals was Edward, prince of Wales, and one of the best Hagen stories—there are many, many good ones—involves the future king of England. "Pull the pin, Eddie," Hagen told the prince when they were standing on a green together, an act of charming impertinence—the English are sensitive to slights of their royal family—that some golf historians (such as Price) claim Hagen never said.

Staying away from that issue, anyone familiar with the larger-than-life life of Walter Hagen must concede that he *could* have said such a thing, and therein lies the key to fully appreciating this grandiose, audacious, wonderfully flamboyant personality. For there can be no denying that he said many outrageous things in his time, such as when he remarked to a bosomy woman in a low-cut dress, "My, what a lovely bunker you'd make," or when his wife happened to notice, as he was undressing for bed, that he wasn't wearing the pair of underpants than he had started out with in the morning. Hagen, it's true, was a bit of a playboy and did not regard the marital bed with the sacredness it is perhaps due.

"My God," he said, clutching his naked bottom with both hands, "I've been robbed!"

Underpants or no, Hagen cut a figure on and off the golf course. He was as sharp a dresser as the staid and formal world of golf had ever seen. He wore silk shirts, custom-made European shoes, argyle socks, and cravats. To maintain a crisp, fresh appearance, he would change his white flannel pants a minimum of twice a day in hot weather. He was a sight, golf's first dandy. At his first appearance at the National Open, in 1913, before he was well known, he wore a rainbow-striped silk shirt, a pair of white flannels (fresh, of course), and white bucks with red rubber soles. The Haig finished fourth that year, the same year that Francis Ouimet shocked the golf establishment with his upset of the two Englishmen, Vardon and Ray. Hagen was twenty at the time, the same as Ouimet.

A former caddie and a school dropout, Walter was a gifted baseballer who thought seriously about trying to play in the major leagues. "My ambition was to make the major leagues," he wrote in his autobiography. "I was firmly convinced that if I were to make a lot of money, it would have to be in baseball." Hagen pitched for his hometown Rochester Ramblers, leading them to three city titles, and he was on the verge of skipping the 1914 Open—the year after he took fourth—for a possible tryout with the Philadelphia Phillies. Fortunately for golf, a Rochester benefactor stepped in and offered to pay Hagen's way to Chicago if he played in the Open. Walter agreed, and returned the kindness by winning the event.

The 1914 Open at Midlothian Country Club was Hagen's coming-out party. While Ouimet, the previous year's winner, showed up and played well, Hagen dusted him and everybody else after suffering through the most famous stomachache in golf history. Even when he was young, Hagen liked to treat himself well. The night before the opening round, he dined on lobster at a posh downtown Chicago restaurant. But the meal gave him intestinal pains and cramps all night long, and he thought seriously about withdrawing from the tournament. He did not, and led the Open all four rounds of play.

In the social structure of that time, golf pros such as Hagen were on the scale of busboys in the eyes of the high-toned members of the country clubs that employed them. "The pro in those days was little more than a servant, an instructor to the rich, a craftsman who fashioned clubs in the quiet of his own quarters," writes Ron Fimrite. Enter Sir Walter, as he was dubbed (he wasn't a knight, he only acted like one). "Such a man bristled at the ridiculous notion that he wasn't good enough to be seen inside a clubhouse," says Fimrite. By walking through the clubhouse doors at Midlothian and at other tournaments later in his career as well, he helped break down the hierarchical class lines of golf society. (There is, of course, still much work to do in this area.)

Out on the course, Hagen was equally refreshing and unstuffy. He was as loosey-goosey as they come. On the 15th fairway of the final day of that Open, he stopped for a moment to chat up a pretty, young girl he had been admiring for the past few holes. Her name was Mabel, and she was anxious to learn how to play golf. Walter said he thought he could help her with that and offered to call her that evening around eight. "Is that all right with you?" he asked. Mabel said that was fine, and Walter went back to the business of pasting the rest of the field in the tournament. He finished at 290, tying what was then a record for low score in the Open, but a local Chicago boy, Chick Evans, was making a run at him on the back nine. Asked if he was nervous about this, Hagen, relaxing in the locker room following his round, said, "Why should I be? I've got *my* score."

The next morning, though—presumably after fixing up a date with pretty Mabel—Hagen got his first attack of the nerves. Suddenly, over breakfast, he blurted out, "Good night! I'm champion of the whole damn country!" Indeed he was. And the best years were yet to come.

Doing the Diegel

◈

The next time you go up to the first tee, think of Leo Diegel and you won't feel as nervous. *Nobody* was as nervous as Leo—on the tee, around the green, or in the clubhouse. Walter Hagen, who was as cool as Leo was jittery, shared a lunch with Diegel after eighteen holes of their 1926 PGA match-play final. After lunch they would go at each other for another eighteen and see who was best.

Leo was full of vapors and superstitions. He believed that no one could beat him in the state of Maryland, and he got upset every year when the major tournaments weren't scheduled there. For the record, his PGA final against Hagen took place on Long Island, but it hardly mattered after they were finished with lunch. For his repast, Diegel ordered tea and toast, while the more robust and freewheeling Hagen had vichyssoise, roast duck, and French champagne. As Hagen reveled, Diegel got sicker and sicker to his stomach until he threw his napkin onto the table, burst from his seat, and walked into a door. Needless to say, Hagen won the match.

You don't hear much about Leo Diegel anymore, but he was a superb golfer for his time—the late 1920s—who won two major titles and might have won still more were it not for a constitution like a Mexican jumping bean. If he could have played even par golf over the last six holes of the 1925 U.S. Open, the title would have been his; he blew up in every way imaginable and shot nine over. Eight years later at the British Open he yipped a gimme putt on the 72nd hole—Leo was the King of Yips—that cost him the chance to be in a playoff for the championship.

In the vain hope of preventing such occurrences, Leo developed a highly unorthodox putting style that Bernard Darwin, the English golf writer, described as "Diegel-ing." It was an elbows-outward stance that looked somewhat like a gooney bird flapping its wings before takeoff. The verb "to Diegel" (as in I Diegel, you Diegel, he, she, or it Diegels) might mean to yip a putt, as Leo did quite often. But it also might mean to exhibit extreme nervousness on the tee, another of poor Leo's characteristics.

Here, it's easy to feel sympathy for him. Nothing is more nerve-racking than that first drive of the day. But such was Diegel's compulsively fretful nature that he took everything beyond the norm.

Playing in the Los Angeles Open one year, he became obsessed with some horse stables located in the out-of-bounds area on the left of the first fairway at the Riviera Country Club. He could not get these stables out of his mind. He dreamed about them, he saw them when he turned a corner on the street. And sure enough, when he went out for his practice round at Riviera, Leo hooked his first drive into those stables.

So on the first day of the tournament, Leo decided to change tactics. Although it meant a penalty stroke against him, he hit his tee shot into the stables . . . *on purpose*. "That takes care of that," he said to himself. "Now I can start playing golf." And his first legitimate drive of the day sailed arrow-straight down the center of the fairway.

The Psych Artist (Walter Hagen—Part II)

For all his reputation as a high liver, Walter Hagen is regarded as one of the two or three best match players ever. One-on-one, mano a mano, the Haig was at his best—perhaps because in match play, as opposed to medal, you play against your opponent rather than seeking to accumulate the lowest number of strokes over a round. This enabled Hagen to go to work against a given individual, and here we need no qualifier: he was the cleverest, most inventive psych artist the game has ever known. In this regard, Hagen is without peer.

He seldom arrived at the first tee of a match on time, forcing his opponent to wait ten, fifteen, twenty-five minutes or more until he showed up. "Doing a Hagen" became a catchphrase for keeping a guy waiting at the tee in order to upset his play. When Hagen did finally make an appearance, it often was in a chauffeur-driven limousine. As to the reason for his tardiness, Hagen might charmingly explain that his chauffeur, poor fellow, had gotten lost in the fog. So what if there was no fog? Details, details.

Dressed in a tuxedo, his black hair slicked down in the style of the time, Hagen looked for all the world as if he had just rolled in from an all-night party. And often he had. A beautiful woman might be seated next to him. Bidding her adieu, he would change into his golfing garb, precipitating further delay, though he might leave his dancing pumps on while playing the first hole. After that he would change into his regular golf shoes, giving his pumps to his caddie. Hagen's act was well known. Gene Sarazen, one of his chief rivals in the 1920s and early 1930s, was determined to get the better of him at least once. Before the PGA Championship one year Hagen did a Hagen, but so did Sarazen, hiding behind a snack stand for a half hour until Sir Walter's entourage appeared. Showing admirable restraint, Sarazen did not make his entrance for another ten minutes, making the man in the tux wait for a change.

Hagen was known to stand at the first tee on the opening round of a tournament and say, "Well, I wonder who's going to take second." Coming from a lesser player, such a boast would have been laughable. But Hagen had the goods to back it up. He was, along with Bobby

Jones, the dominant player of his era, though Jones is far better known today. Jones's affiliation with the Masters helps perpetuate his name, while the large and flamboyant figure of Walter Hagen seems to have shrunk over time.

Nor have today's tight-cheeked golf analysts been kind to him in their assessment of his swing, which was sort of "a sway and a lurch" when he was young and never did smooth out even as he was winning all those Opens and PGAs. His was not a classic swing à la Mr. Jones; Hagen, heresy upon heresies, even moved his head! But he was nifty with the irons and carried a shoot-'em-dead putter, and his supreme self-confidence brought him through the tight spots. In the 1924 British Open, after improvising his way around the Hoylake course, he faced an eight-foot putt on 18 to win. Hagen, as was his wont, did not linger; did not yip. He went up and knocked it into the center of the cup.

"You seemed to treat that putt rather casually," said a writer. "Did you know you had it to win?"

"Sure I knew I had it to win," said Hagen dismissively. "But no man ever beat *me* in a playoff."

In other words, if he had missed the putt and gone into a playoff, he would simply have beaten his opponent then. So why sweat a lousy eight-footer?

This was Hagen at his most cunning. Confident, relaxed, unhurried, and unworried. "I've never played a perfect eighteen holes," he was quoted as saying. "There is no such thing. I expect to make at least seven mistakes a round. Therefore, when I make a bad shot, I don't worry about it. It's just one of the seven." Another Hagen maxim: "Make the hard shots look easy and the easy shots look hard." It was all part of the mind game he played on his opponents.

Hagen won his second U.S. Open in 1919, whipping Mike Brady in an 18-hole playoff after they had tied in regulation. To make it into the playoff Hagen needed to sink a six-foot putt on the final green at Brae Burn in West Newton, Massachusetts. But before taking the putt he insisted on calling Brady out of the locker room to witness the event for himself. Brady was given a chair, and with the flourish of a great stage actor, the Haig drilled it.

That evening Walter attended a party in Boston for Al Jolson—the two were pals, of course—and as the festivities rolled into the early morning hours, somebody asked Hagen if perhaps he shouldn't get some rest because Brady would surely be home in bed. "He may be in bed," said Walter with a wink, "but he won't be asleep." By dawn Hagen returned to his hotel room and after breakfast and a shower, arrived at Brae Burn in his Pierce Arrow sedan. True to his nervous temperament, Brady was already out on the practice tee hitting balls. (Hagen disdained practice; said it made his game stale.) After they both parred the first hole, Hagen reached into his bag of tricks on the second tee and came up with this:

"Mike, if I were you, I'd roll down my shirtsleeves."

"Why?" asked Brady.

"Well," said Hagen, "the way it is now, everyone in the gallery can see your muscles quivering when you hit." Quivering or not, Brady muscled his drive into the trees and bogeyed the hole. Hagen won the playoff by a stroke.

People claimed that Hagen intentionally mismarked his clubs—made his 7-iron an 8, and so on—in order to mislead his opponents. Whether true or not, Hagen seems certainly capable of such tactics. For him, gamesmanship was part of the game. As a full-time golf professional—the first ever—he wanted to win not only for the titles and the prestige, but because he needed the money. A U.S. or British Open looked good on his résumé, and what's more, it jacked up his appearance fees, just as it does for the pros of today. Plain and simple, Walter needed the dough. There were all those parties, the wealthy and famous in attendance, alimony to pay to his ex-wives, girlfriends, European clothes, the laundry expenses, the limousine driver who needed his money—Walter led a very complicated life. At the 1927 PGA, he received his winner's check in the basement of the club so as to avoid the bill collectors waiting upstairs.

Still, Hagen lived (and played) dauntlessly. He never failed to heed the Oscar Wilde maxim that you should take care of the luxuries because the necessities always take care of themselves. At the 1920 British Open, Hagen stayed at the Ritz Hotel in London and appeared at the golf course in a Austro-Daimler limousine with a footman. On a later visit to Britain he chartered an airplane to fly him to an inn forty miles away from the course because, he said, the food at the clubhouse where the golfers were supposed to stay was inferior. It's true that Hagen made these gestures in part as a protest against British snobbishness and their treatment of golf pros as a subservient class. But even in protest, Hagen was true to himself. He loved grand gestures. Grand, expensive gestures. And the aura that surrounded him worked to his advantage on the golf course.

In 1926, Hagen beat Bobby Jones in a 72-hole, one-on-one match. Afterward he spent $1,000 of his $8,000 prize money on diamond cuff links for his rival. Some years later, when he was captaining the U.S. Ryder Cup team, a tailor asked him how much he could spend on the team's uniforms. "Whatever is necessary," said Hagen. "Think nothing of it." That was Hagen, all right: when it came to money, think nothing of it.

The idea of a gallery—people paying money to see a golfer golf—began with Hagen. People loved him, and a golf match was not so serious that he did not have a moment to chat with friends or others who came to see him play. Once in a big match a dog suddenly bolted across the green and snatched the ball in its teeth just as Hagen was about to putt. After the dog was captured and the ball returned to the spot where it had been, Hagen coolly nailed the putt. "Why should I be upset?" he said when asked if the incident had bothered him. "It was the same putt, wasn't it?"

One last Hagen story, one last grand gesture. Down two strokes to Bob Jones on the 72nd hole of the 1926 British Open, Hagen stood about 150 yards from the pin. In order to tie Jones and force a playoff, he needed to hole out on this, his second, shot. It was an impossible task, of course, but that did not dissuade the Haig from giving it his theatrical all. Before hitting, he walked all the way to the green and asked that the pin be pulled.

"Pull the pin, please."

The pin was pulled, and Sir Walter slowly and dramatically walked back to his ball. He did not make the shot, but such was the wonder of the Hagen personality that no one doubted for a second that he could have.

Emperor Jones

Bobby Jones played, as Mike Royko has noted, in the days "when a golfer wore a visor to keep the sun out of his eyes, not to sell fairway condos." He was a contemporary of Walter Hagen's, but a far different breed of cat: he was an amateur. Nowadays "amateur" is practically a dirty word, what you call a person who can't do the job the way

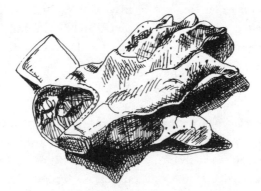

it should be done. But in Jones's time it signified a man or woman who measured success not only by what he did on the golf course, but also by what he did off it. When Jones quit tournament golf in 1930, he said he wanted "to avoid getting myself into such a position that I would have to keep on playing." Quitting, he added, kept "golf in its proper perspective, a means of obtaining recreation and enjoyment."

Jones was twenty-eight when he hung up his clubs, a mere boy by contemporary sporting standards. Of course, in his day there was almost no money to be had in the professional game. The U.S. Open paid a measly five hundred dollars to the winner, pocket change to today's pros.

A classic question involving Jones is: Was he the greatest of all time? "To my generation Jones will always be the greatest," answers Henry Longhurst, who saw everybody from Jones to Nicklaus. Herbert Warren Wind, another venerable and esteemed golf observer, weighs in with a vote for Bobby: "It took Bobby many seasons and many heartaches before he learned to stop worrying about what the other fellow was doing and to pit his skill against the proper opponent, Old Man Par. When he finally learned this lesson, there was no one who could stay anyplace close to Bobby Jones." It was Jones himself,

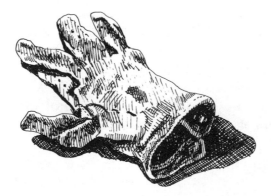

an eminently commonsensical man, who put this question into the right perspective: "All that a man can do is to beat those who are around when he is around. He cannot beat those who went before or those who are yet to come."

And make no mistake: young Bobby whipped the pants off just about everybody around. He entered twenty-seven majors in his career and won thirteen of them. He won three of the four British Opens he entered, and in the decade of the twenties, his showcase years, he owned the U.S. Open lock, stock, and barrel. He finished second in 1922, first in 1923, second in 1924 and again in 1925, first in 1926, second in 1928, and first in 1929 and 1930. This last Open was the third leg in his famous Grand Slam, which then consisted of the U.S. and British Opens, the British Amateur, and the U.S. Amateur, another event he claimed as his personal property. Understandably, as the saying goes, "it was Jones against the field." When he was in a tournament, the other players were haunted by the question: What is Jones doing? His score was the benchmark, the one you had to beat in order to win.

His chief competitor was Walter Hagen, and their differing personalities and roles formed a kind of yin and yang of golf: Jones, the modest and proper amateur, versus Hagen, the freewheeling pro. Comparing the two at golf, Gene Sarazen, who played against them both, gives the nod to Mr. Jones: "In their one man-against-man meeting in Florida in 1926," writes Sarazen, "Walter administered a decisive lacing to Bob, but it is notable that Walter never was able to win an Open championship in which Jones was entered. Walter had Jonesitis as bad as the rest of us."

Stories about the best golfers of today—the American ones, at any rate—fit a predictable pattern: they started young, played in college, struggled for a few years after joining the pros, etc. Jones can't be pigeonholed in the same way. There's more to his résumé than golf. He was a mechanical engineer. He earned an English-literature degree at Harvard and with the guidance of his friend the journalist O. B. Keeler, wrote a syndicated newspaper column. He kept scrupulous notebooks and diaries about the matches he played and once estimated that he had written a half million words on golf, including a collection, *Bob Jones on Golf*, edited by Charles Price, which is one of the best golf books ever. After retiring from the game Jones starred in a series of Hollywood-produced instructional films, *How I Play Golf*, and later, *How to Break 90*, which have been rereleased on videocassette and are considered classics of the genre, worth viewing today. Like his father, Jones was a lawyer. He was also a successful businessman who designed golf clubs for A.G. Spalding and Brothers. In his most lasting contribution to the game, he helped found that yearly springtime tribute to magnolias and azaleas, the Masters, and codesigned the place where it is played, Augusta National. The only modern golfer with a résumé that can compete with Jones's is Jack Nicklaus, who, in fact, idolized the Georgia native and patterned his approach to the game after him.

Indeed, Nicklaus and Jones have many similarities. Both were boy golfing prodigies and perhaps a little pampered at that. Jones started playing at five. At nine, he won a junior golf championship in Atlanta, beating a boy seven years older. Young Bobby, though not a large fellow, was a fine natural athlete who could play all the sports. But after he journeyed north to Brookline, Massachusetts, and got turned on watching Francis Ouimet beat the Englishmen in the 1913 Open, he would be distracted no more. In the fall of 1913, at age eleven, he shot an 80. Two years later he shot a 73 in a tournament. The next year, he carded a 69.

At fourteen, Jones had already formed a reputation as a gifted golfer, no matter what the age. At the 1916 Amateur in Merion he was beaten in the third round by the defending champion, but made quite an impression anyway. "Improvement?" said Walter Travis, the former Amateur champion, when asked what the boy wonder could do to improve his game. "He can never improve his shots, if that's what you mean. But he will learn a good deal more about playing them."

Considering how young and gifted he was, it's not surprising that young Bob had some behavior problems on the golf course. Behavior problems? He was the John McEnroe of golf, a snarling, hissing, club-throwing little brat. Jones expected perfection from himself, and when he did not achieve it, he blew sky-high. Playing in an exhibition with Alexa Stirling, the women's champion, the tempestuous tyke threw a fit and with it his clubs and his ball. Some were not amused. "I read the pity in Alexa's soft brown eyes," Jones said later, "and I finally settled down, but not before I had made a complete fool of myself." This salutary chastening is part of the Jones legend. So is his eventual transformation into a model of golfing decorum. From bad boy to hero—it's kind of a Tom Sawyer story for golfers.

Although Tom, and certainly his buddy Huck, would've thought Jones carried the goody two-shoes stuff to extremes. When he was a young spitfire, Jones might play thirty-six holes as a warm-up the day before a tournament. As he got older, worn down by the pressures of always being the man to beat, he would relax the day before with a good book. One of his favorites was Papini's *Life of Christ*. Before his 1929 Open playoff with Al Espinosa, Jones asked tournament officials if they would delay the starting time so that Espinosa could attend Mass. (Jones himself became a Roman Catholic before his death in 1971.) At an Open four years earlier Jones penalized himself a stroke when his ball made a microscopically small movement at address. The stroke cost him the title, though he won praise for his good sportsmanship. Such compliments made him bristle. "There is only one way to play the game," he said. "You might as well praise a man for not robbing a bank."

Jones's breakthrough as a major-tournament golfer occurred at the 1923 U.S. Open when he beat Bobby Cruikshank in a playoff. This began his mature phase, which culminated seven years later with his Grand Slam and his subsequent retirement. "There could be no more fascinating player to watch," wrote Bernard Darwin at the time, "not only for the rhythmic character of his swing but for the swiftness with which he played." Jones had an enviably short preswing routine:

right foot set, left set, into the backswing. "One might as well attempt to describe the smoothness of the wind as to paint a clear picture of his golf swing," writes another admirer, Grantland Rice. His putting procedure was as purposeful as the other parts of his game: set the putter in front of the ball, then in back of it, then *thonk!* into the cup. Bobby's putter, which he dubbed "Calamity Jane," featured two black bands around the shaft. The club had been broken during one of his youthful temper tantrums, and the bands held the shaft together. But such was his popularity that Jones wanna-be's around the country copied him by taping two black bands around their putters.

Jones was known as the Mechanical Man, stemming from his machinelike consistency. "If you keep shooting pars at them," he said once, "they all crack sooner or later." At Sunningdale, outside London, in a qualifying round for the British Open, his unwavering constancy produced what has been described as the "perfect" round of golf. He shot a 66—33 strokes to the green, 33 putts. Thirty-three on the front nine, 33 on the back. No 5s or 2s, every hole a 3 or a 4. They didn't call him Emperor Jones—another of his nicknames— for nothing.

The last act in Jones's life came after his retirement from golf and is imbued with the unalterable sadness of disease and dying. Jones, a frail child who could not take solid foods until he was five, contracted a crippling spinal disease in his later years. He lost the use of his arms and legs and by the late forties, was making his annual appearance at the Masters in a wheelchair. Up until then, though, Jones played in his own tournament and in selected exhibitions. The most famous of those exhibitions occurred in 1936, when Jones traveled to Europe to see the Berlin Olympics. Afterward he stopped in Scotland, and when word got around that he was going to play a round of golf at St. Andrews, more than two thousand people came to watch. "I shall never forget that round," said Jones. "It was not anything like a serious golf match. There was a sort of holiday mood in the crowd."

The holiday was in seeing Jones play. He had won both the British

Open and the British Amateur at St. Andrews, and the people there knew him and embraced him as one of their own. They cheered his every shot. Jones got around the front nine in 32, but his score could have been twice that and it's likely no one would have cared. The joy was in being out there and in seeing Jones play just like in the old days, and when he swung it was almost as if the years had fallen away and you were young again and nothing had changed and Jones was still the greatest in the world. On the 10th hole he hit a blind tee shot onto the green a few feet from the pin. The gallery roared in delight, and his ten-year-old caddie, flushed with admiration, said, "My, but you're a wonder, sir!" In all his years of golf Jones said he had never received a finer compliment.

St. Andrews

In 1958, suffering from the muscular disease that would later take his life, Bobby Jones paid a last visit to St. Andrews, the ancient Scottish golf town that had meant so much to him personally. Thirty-seven years earlier, in his first British Open, the teenaged hothead had torn up his scorecard in disgust and in the most cowardly of golfing acts, stormed off the Old Course and withdrew from the tournament. A mature Jones would look back on that day as a turning point in his life. The shame he felt in withdrawing from the greatest tournament in the world, coupled with the embarrassment of his poor play, prompted him to reassess his life and make a change for the better.

By 1958, Jones had been out of competitive golf for nearly thirty years, but the golf-mad citizenry of St. Andrews had not forgotten him. They paid him their highest honor, naming him a "Burgess and Guild Brother" of the town with all the rights and privileges accorded such a lofty post. The last American to be so honored was a bloke named Ben Franklin.

Jones's speech to an assembly of St. Andrews townspeople is among the most moving in all of the literature of golf. Relegated by this time to a wheelchair, there was hardly a dry eye in the house as he spoke: "My thoughts are not of championships and trophies as I stand here tonight. You people possess a sensibility which causes you to be able to extend cordiality and express friendliness in the most ingenious ways. I could take out of my life everything except my experiences at St. Andrews and I'd still have a rich, full life." When he was done, the townspeople broke into an old Scottish song: "Will Ye No' Come Back Again?" But he never did.

St. Andrews, the golf capital of the world, is a tiny summer resort town located on the Firth of Forth on the gusty eastern coast of Scotland. It has a cathedral and a university dating from 1413, the oldest in the country. The Black Bull and Bailie Glass's House are two of the taverns in town, places to go after an outing on the links. What gives St. Andrews its special charm is not its golf courses per se, but the way in which golf is an essential feature of the daily warp and woof of town life. "It is delightful to see a whole town given up to golf," wrote Bernard Darwin in the early part of this century, though it is no less true of St. Andrews today. "To see the butcher and the baker and the candlestick maker shouldering his clubs as soon as his day's work is done and making a dash for the links . . . It is that utter abandonment to golf that gives the place its attractiveness."

St. Andrews, adds Tony Jacklin, "breathes golf from every pore of its ancient buildings." One of those old buildings is home to the Royal and Ancient Golf Club, the most famous golf club in the world. The Royal and Ancient is the rule-making body for Britain and all the world except the United States and Mexico, where the USGA prevails. Its headquarters is a weathered, gray-stone building that sits astride the Old Course at St. Andrews, and its membership rolls have included some of the most storied names in golf, past and present. But the old building could fall down tomorrow and golf would continue to be played in St. Andrews, as it has, for centuries.

The Royal and Ancient does not manage the four courses of St. Andrews: Eden, Jubilee, New, and Old. These are operated by a public trust, and they are all open to the public. But they are nothing like the courses you will find in the United States. On the Old Course, the place where the British Open is played when it comes to St. Andrews, there is nothing that can be described as a "fairway," at least in the sense we understand the term. Not a tree is to be found anywhere, and the plain, windswept landscape hardly seems fit for livestock, let alone golf. Ancient stone walls and rutted paths pock the course. There are seven huge double greens, and the tee shot on 11 must cross over the so-called fairway on 7. No golf-course architect in his right mind would design a course like the Old Course today. Its principal architects, in fact, were the wind, the sea, and hungry sheep. "In the beginning it knew no architect but nature," said Pat Ward-Thomas, a British writer. "It came into being by evolution rather than design, and with no other course is the hand of man less evident."

Golf, in its earliest forms, had nothing to do with private clubs, class bias, or even golf courses. Golf was a cross-country game played in open fields by the sea. "Links," in essence, is the word for the sand dunes found along the Scottish coast. The everyday people of Scotland were playing for hundreds of years before private golf clubs were formed, the first being the Honorable Company of Edinburgh Golfers, in 1744, followed ten years later by the Royal and Ancient. The Old Course remains a monument to the early classless days of golf, before the rise of private clubs permanently altered the social landscape of the game.

Goethe said that when you walk through the streets of Paris, you walk through history. Well, when you walk the Old Course, you walk through golf history. There, on that tricky par-3 11th, is where young Jones pulled his famous fit. After two respectable rounds in the '21 Open, he took a 46 on the front nine and on 11, got trapped in a bunker. Four swings later, his ball still in the trap, Jones stormed off in rage. Young Tom Morris was a phenom of an earlier time, the greatest player in the world in the middle 1800s until his untimely death at age twenty-four. His bones are interred on a hill on the Old Course. Cross the stone bridge o'er Swilcan Burn and you will be hard upon the most famous final green in golf. On that green, with the majestic clubhouse of the Royal and Ancient looming over him, Doug Sanders missed a three-foot putt that would have clinched the 1970 Open. Sanders then lost the title in a playoff to Jack Nicklaus. After yipping that putt Sanders would probably have liked to crawl in and join Young Tom.

When you play the rolling, seaside Old Course, you must not only prepare for winds strong enough to pick up Dorothy's house and move it to Oz, you must also learn a new language. A creek is not a creek in Scotland; it's a "burn." Swilcan Burn is the Rae's Creek of St. Andrews. "Gorse" is a gnarly shrub that regards golf balls much the way a Venus flytrap regards insects. Due to the wind you have to shoot low and stay close to the ground, but you've got to be able to get it up, too. The wind changes from day to day, sometimes from front nine to back nine, and it's a marvel. A Belgian pro in a British Open long ago was facing a twenty-foot putt downhill with the wind behind him. He hit the ball *uphill*; it rolled up and turned around and, pushed by the wind, went ten feet past the hole.

The Old Course, says one of its admirers, Tom Watson, is filled with "misdirection and blindness." You cannot aim for the pin in the normal way; in many cases you do not have any idea where the pin is. You shoot over knolls and sand traps, or you aim at church spires or hotels in town, heeding always the advice of your caddie. The pros at the British Open are lucky; they can use the television towers at each green to line up their shots. The rest of us—heaven help us—must rely on our wits. "There is always a way at St. Andrews, although it is not always the obvious way," wrote an older and wiser Bob Jones, who came back to win an Open on the Old Course after his boyish upset. This may sound a little mysterious, but the Old Course is a little mysterious itself, a crumbling haunted house of a golf course swept by those eerie Scottish mists from which you halfway expect Heathcliff to emerge, clutching Catherine to his bosom.

At St. Andrews, the bunkers have the most descriptive of names: Hell Bunker, Coffins, Cat's Trap, Lion's Mouth, Walkinshaw's Grave, the Principal's Nose. Some of the bunkers open like the jaws of the abyss; others are just big enough to fit "an angry man and his niblick," in Bernard Darwin's telling phrase. The most famous bunker is on 17, the legendary Road Hole. It is a pot bunker that rims the left of the green. In 1978 it proved the downfall of Tommy Nakajima, who, two strokes off the Open lead, got caught in the bunker. It took him four chopping, lunging, exasperating strokes to get out, and he carded a nine on the hole, killing his chances. Henceforth the bunker has been known as the Sands of Nakajima.

But the Road Hole, widely regarded as the most difficult par 4 in tournament golf, has been the downfall of many another golfer as well. "The reason it's such a tough par four is that it's a par five," explains Ben Crenshaw. It begins with a drive past the Old Course Hotel on your right; this area is out-of-bounds. Then it's a long iron up to a green guarded by the Road Bunker on the left and a road —a road!—behind it. The road is in play.

The 17th tripped up Arnold Palmer in his quest for a 1960 Open title and a possible Grand Slam bid. He played it poorly over the course of the four days, and the strokes he lost there cost him the tournament. A quarter of a century later Tom Watson lost his chance for a sixth British Open title (and first at St. Andrews) when his 2-iron approach overshot the green and rolled onto the road. Cramped by the wall that runs alongside it, Watson made a difficult chip out and salvaged a tough bogey, but Seve Ballesteros made par and then birdied 18, and that was that. Ballesteros was champion, Watson was runner-up, and another layer of legend was added to the crusty annals of the Old Course at St. Andrews.

Down Days in the Land of Tradition

"Tradition!"

The song sung by Tevye and the other townspeople in *Fiddler on the Roof* could as easily apply to the British and their golf. The British are full of it. Tradition, that is.

Sam Snead found that out when he appeared in his first and only British Open in 1946. Trying to get a feel for the layout of the place, Snead took a walking tour of the Old Course at St. Andrews prior to the start of the tournament. When he came to one of those huge double greens, the Scottish-born caddie accompanying him pointed out where the pin placements were going to be.

"How do you know they'll put the pin there?" Snead wondered.

"Because that's where they've put it for fifty years," replied the caddie.

Indeed. If it was good enough for the British fifty years ago, it's good enough for them today. The American view, on the other hand, tends to be somewhat different, as Snead himself showed earlier in that week. On the train coming into St. Andrews, the native Virginian leaned over to a British gentleman sitting next to him and asked what that nondescript-looking pasture was. "Why, that's the home of the Royal and Ancient Golf Club, founded in 1754," said the gentleman. "Well, back home we wouldn't plant cow beets on land like that," said Snead. These comments got wide play in Great Britain and caused the kind of stink that the Fleet Street press is famous for. "Snead, a rural American type, undoubtedly would think the Leaning Tower of Pisa a structure about to totter and crash at his feet," sniffed the *Times* of London.

Snead's comments were seen as an attack on the most hallowed of all golfing grounds, as well as being disrespectful of tradition. In the eyes of the British (or some British anyhow), thumbing your nose at tradition is second only to insulting the Queen as a crime against God and country.

What must've rankled the Scots still more about Snead's remarks—the salt in the wound, as it were—was the fact that that ole hick could whip the pants off any of their countrymen in the game they invented. The barbarians had stormed the Temple of Golf and run up the Stars 'n' Stripes. Actually, the Americans were such ignorant clods they couldn't even appreciate what they were doing. They didn't play golf for history's sake. So they stayed home, where the money and the best competition were, and they left the British to pick the cobwebs off the trophy cases in the Royal and Ancient. Snead made one appearance at the British. He won. Hogan made an appearance. He won. Most of their peers couldn't be bothered. Golf had come full circle. By midcentury America had become the center of the golf world, and the Land of Tradition had turned into Nowheresville.

Still, it was not as bleak in Britain as all that. England could rightly claim the greatest golf writer of the first half-century (Bernard Darwin, grandson of the naturalist Charles) and its funniest humorist (the inestimable P. G. Wodehouse). The pickings among players were a little slimmer, but there were some notables, foremost among them Henry Cotton, a tall, graceful swinger who won the 1934 British

Open but whose best years were taken away by World War II. Cotton was the finest English male golfer since Vardon and a match for the Americans. Dapper and polished as an adult, he knew his mind as a child. At his London school, he was a dedicated cricket player until he got into a dispute with his headmaster, who recommended a caning for his insubordination. Young Henry did not cotton to this and said he would not sit still for it. In that case, said the headmaster, you shall never play cricket again. "In that case," said the boy, "I will play golf." Good for you, Henry!

Max Faulkner was another British golfer of this era, and a wonderfully cocksure one he was. While leading a British Open in the early fifties he began signing autographs "Max Faulkner, British Open Champion," though there were still two rounds to go. Fortunately for Max, he held on to win. At another point, commenting on his putting, Mad Max said, "Four-footers? I shall never miss another of those." One somehow thinks that Max had a little harder time making good on this pledge.

A less appetizing personality belonged to one Archie Compston, as vainglorious a golfer as ever lived. He played for the British Ryder Cup team in the late 1920s and 1930s, but his talents never quite matched his high opinion of himself. How could they? He was the very definition of a stuffed shirt, intolerant of his supposed "inferiors," a man who needed three caddies because one could not possibly meet all his needs. He smoked as he played, and between shots one of his caddies would hold his burning cigarette and then return it to him after he hit. Old Archie was a pain in the butt even to his countrymen, and while giving a lesson to the marchioness of Northampton, he so infuriated her with his high-handed uppityness that she turned on him with an 8-iron, whacking him across the shins. "You've got it! You've got it!" screamed Archie as he hopped away holding his shin. "Now hit the golf ball the same way!"

A Short Man's Game

Unlike in sports such as football or basketball, where you generally need to be a massive physical specimen to play in the pros, a person of less than average height and weight can thrive in golf. Bob Jones was only five foot eight. Of more contemporary vintage, such names as Ian Woosnam (5-4½), Jeff Sluman (5-7, 133 lbs.), Tom Kite (5-8), and Corey Pavin (5-9, 140 lbs.) come to mind. On today's Senior Tour, Gary Player (5-7, 150 lbs.), Chi Chi Rodriguez (5-7, 135 lbs.), and Lee Trevino (5-7) are a few more in this category.

Ben Hogan was five nine, two inches taller than Bob Toski, who tipped the scales at 127 pounds. Toski, nowadays known as one of the game's leading teachers, was the top money-winner on the 1954 Tour. His fellow pros joked that Toski was the only guy who needed a lifeguard to take a shower. Ernest Jones, another famous golf teacher, though from a different era, was five five and a half and 130 pounds.

Paul Runyan, who was five seven and a half, won the PGA championship in 1934 and again in 1938. Both victories came against men who could easily outdrive him. In a magazine interview a few years ago, Little Poison, as he was called, said he thought short people had certain advantages over the bigger hitters, notably the ability to get their goat in pressure situations. "Long hitters often tighten up at the prospect of losing to someone who is small or can't hit the ball far," he said. "It's an ego thing." It helps, too, if you're as gifted around the greens as Runyan was.

In the 1938 PGA, which was then a match-play event, Runyan faced Sam Snead, one of the longest hitters on the tour. Snead's drives regularly traveled fifty yards beyond Runyan's, and on a long par 5, Runyan would need three shots to cover the same distance as his opponent's two. But like all shorter players, Little Poison found ways to compensate. He sunk a sixty-foot putt at one point. At another critical juncture in the match a shot of Snead's came to rest on the green between Runyan's ball and the hole. This was in the days of the "stymie" rule, when you couldn't mark the ball, so Runyan had to make do.

This was an ironic development, for Snead had profited in his previous match from a similar situation. After he missed a short putt on the 14th green, his ball had stopped in front of the hole, blocking the line of his opponent, Jimmy Hines. Hines chipped his ball up, but as it was going into the hole, it tipped Snead's in, too. The stroke Snead gained here helped him reach the finals against Runyan.

But the gods of golf—abetted by Runyan's consummate skill— were not about to smile on Snead twice. Runyan pulled a wedge from his bag and hopped his ball over Snead's into the cup on the fly. He won the match by one of the most lopsided margins in PGA history.

Mr. Double Eagle: Gene Sarazen

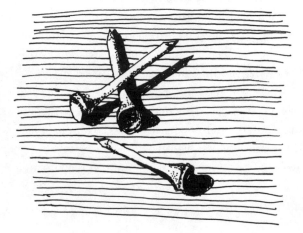

When you talk about short guys who could play the game, one name must be at the top of the list: Gene Sarazen. He was five foot five inches tall, and as cocky as they come. He won all the great titles, while pulling off the single most famous golf shot of all time. A relentlessly hard worker (much like another short stuff, Gary Player), Sarazen believed in health and physical conditioning (again, like Player) as a way to make up for a lack of size. He built up his arms and legs and wielded a fifteen-ounce driver that much larger men could not handle. His power stroke was just that—"a tremendous, elementary thump," in the words of Henry Longhurst, who so admired Sarazen's explosive swing that whenever too many thoughts and theories intruded on his own game, Longhurst would picture Sarazen on the tee and it would lift him out of his slump.

If you see a picture of Sarazen in his prime—not swinging, just relaxing—you can get a sense of what kind of player he was. There's a nice shot of him standing with his longtime rival, Walter Hagen, and he's leaning jauntily against his golf club. He has on a tie, a sweater, and his trademark knickers. His hair is black and slicked down. He's looking slightly to one side and he's smiling, as if he knows a secret he's unwilling to share with the rest of us. There's an air of youthful braggadocio about him, and the message it's sending to others seems unmistakable: "Go ahead. Just try and beat *me*."

Sarazen was one of the fiercest competitors the gentlemanly game of golf has ever seen. "Your game counts for you and mine for me," he was known to say to his fellow competitors. "In other words, look out for number one." He was cocky, brusque, openly ambitious. More than one person has said that Sarazen only talked to people who could personally do him good. In his breakthrough 1922 U.S. Open, Sarazen, then unknown, finished at 288 and had to wait for everyone else to come in. As the field began to close in, a worried friend came up to him and said it looked as if his total was in danger of being topped. Sarazen took the news in stride. "I've got mine," he said. "Let them get theirs." They got theirs, and it wasn't enough. Sarazen was the champ.

Growing up in New York and Connecticut, Sarazen nearly died at fifteen from pneumonia. When he emerged from the hospital, the doctor recommended lots of fresh air and outdoor work, which suited him just fine. Up to then he had worked as a carpenter's helper, and his Italian-immigrant father had discouraged his attempts to play golf, equating it with laziness and goofing off. But after winning a tournament Gene knew he had found not only the key to good health, but the way to make a name for himself. After seeing his given name (Eugenio Saraceni) in the newspaper, the young, upper-aspiring golfer changed it to the one we know him by today.

Ego—not to mention the sand wedge, which he invented during his down years to help his poor bunker game—was certainly an ingredient in Sarazen's success. After his early triumphs he suffered through a decade-long dry spell that ended, at last, in 1932 with victories in both the British and U.S. Opens. Going nearly ten years without a major win might have broken a lesser golfer, but not the self-confident Sarazen. He was a pit bull of a player, always on the attack, always taking risks. He swung so hard with his heavy-hitting driver that occasionally he lost his balance. The journalist O. B. Keeler, observing Sarazen, said that he "gives the impression of straining at the leash." He also played quickly, sometimes a bit too quickly for the people ahead of him. During a practice round in the thirties Sarazen kept hitting drives into a foursome that contained Lloyd Mangrum, who later won a pair of Purple Hearts fighting the Nazis. Finally, Mangrum got fed up and charged back up the fairway where Sarazen was standing. "Mr. Sarazen," Mangrum said, "if you do that one more time, I'm going to hit a ball right down your fucking throat." Mr. Sarazen slowed his game down at that point.

It's impossible to discuss Sarazen's career without discussing (a) his knickers and (b) his famous double eagle. Holing that 4-wood from 265 yards out on the 15th hole at Augusta virtually won him the 1935 Masters (he beat Craig Wood in a playoff), sent sales of 4-woods soaring, and followed him wherever he went in his long, productive golf-playing life. He may have changed his name from Eugenio to Gene, but the public tagged him forever as Mr. Double Eagle. As for those knickers, his fellow pros used to joke that Sarazen wore them so much he went to bed in them.

The most poignant moment in Sarazen's career is told in one of Herbert Warren Wind's collections. At the 1928 British Open at Royal St. George's in England, struggling to be a major player again, Sarazen disobeyed his caddie's advice on what club to use on a crucial hole. The mistake cost him dearly, and he blew up on the hole and lost the title. The caddie's name was Skip Daniels. Daniels, in his late sixties, wore a cap and a wrinkled black oxford suit. He was nearly blind, but he knew Royal St. George's better than any man alive, having patrolled it on foot during World War I when the British feared a German attack. As the two men were saying good-bye, a humbled Sarazen admitted that he had made a mistake and that he should have listened to his caddie's instructions.

"We'll try it again, sir, won't we?" said Skip Daniels.

"I swear," said Sarazen, fighting tears, "that before I die I'm going to win an Open championship for you."

Four years later, his game rejuvenated, Sarazen came back to England and with Daniels as his caddie, won the British Open. A few months later, following a brief illness, Skip Daniels was dead.

Babe Zaharias

Ironically, considering the trouble that the Ladies Professional Golf Association has had in gaining respectability, the greatest all-around athlete in the history of the game was a woman, Babe Didrickson Zaharias. Every father would be proud to have a son like the Babe. She got her nickname—her given name was Mildred—because as a girl, she could hit a baseball like Babe Ruth (or so they said in her hometown). She could also punt a football seventy-five yards, play a smashing game of tennis, swim and dive, and run on a treadmill while playing a harmonica.

"There was nothing Babe could not do and do well," Sarah Ballard writes. In the 1932 National AAU Track and Field Championships, which served as the Olympic Trials as well, Babe, then nineteen, won five of the ten events in the meet—80-meter hurdles, baseball throw, shot put, long jump, and javelin—and set three world records. She captured the team trophy by herself. At the Olympics later in the year, she took gold medals in the hurdles and the javelin. The day after the Olympics she played a friendly round of golf with sportswriter Grantland Rice, who was so taken with her talents that he beseeched her to take up the game full-time. The Babe did indeed do just that, and women's golf—all women's sports, in fact—was changed forever.

Women's golf, like women's everything else, faced considerable resistance in its early years from the men who controlled and dominated the sport. The tradition of women in golf dates from the late 1500s and Mary Queen of Scots, who caused a scandal by playing in public shortly after her husband's death. But the ancient Scots were never keen on the idea of women playing golf, whether their husbands were dead or not. A fantastic piece of gossip survives from the 1800s about a woman golfer, Dame Margaret Ross, who was accused of being a witch. It was said that she used her witchly powers to sabotage the games of her enemies, transforming herself into a golf ball and deliberately rolling off line whenever they putted. Dame Margaret was a good person to have on your side, though. If she liked you, goes the story, she could use her black art to help you sink a twenty-footer.

At the end of the last century and the beginning of this one, women became somewhat more accepted in golf, though they generally played on shorter courses separate from the men's. It's been argued by some that the entry of women into games such as tennis and golf, and their corresponding feelings of self-empowerment, helped fuel the rise in women's political power that culminated, in the United States, with the establishment of the right to vote in 1920. Still, there were any number of obstacles faced by women golfers of the time, not the least of which were the attitudes of men. Writing in the influential *Badminton Library of Sports and Pastimes*, published in 1890, a Lord Wellwood makes the case that it won't be long before "a claim of women's absolute equality in golf be made." But, he adds, "it will be convenient to consider the delicate question under three heads: (1) the abstract right of women to play golf at all; (2) their right to play the 'long round' with or without male companions; and (3) their right to accompany matches as spectators."

To his credit, Lord Wellwood gives a rousing affirmative to the right of women to play golf, but he wasn't quite sure he wanted them hanging around cluttering up things when the men were playing. "At other times—must we say it—they are in the way," said Wellwood. This attitude was hardly exclusive to Britain. In the States, women could play only at certain times and on certain days stipulated by men, and they were denied access to the clubs by the male membership—a policy, sad to say, that continues to this day.

But the prohibitions put on women golfers were not entirely men's doing. Turn-of-the-century fashion for women included corsets, ankle-length skirts, funny hats with feathers, starched collars, and sleeves—not the sort of attire that encourages free and easy athletic movement. By the 1920s and 1930s, things had not gotten much better. "Any glimpse of the ball, quite apart from swinging, was a matter of extreme uncertainty," said Joyce Wethered, who, despite the handicap, had a widely admired swing. Long-sleeved white shirts and tweed coats with calf-length dresses were standard golf-course wear. When it got hot, women could take their coats off, but not roll up their sleeves. It simply wasn't done.

Wethered, a Britisher who was just under six feet tall, was the best player in the world in her day. She won almost everything she entered, scoring in the low and mid-70s when most other women could not break 80. She and her American counterpart, Glenna Collett, and a few others showed that women were capable of an accurate, highly skilled game that, in many crucial respects, was the equal of a man's.

Enter the Babe. Born in Port Arthur, Texas (the same hometown as Janis Joplin), she was cut from a different cloth than her more genteel predecessors. "Are you asking me if I wear girdles and bras and the rest of that junk?" she said to a reporter once. "What do you think I am? A sissy?" On another occasion, when asked how she hit a driver so far, she responded, "I just loosen my girdle and let the ball have it."

Babe's game was power—a quality men could admire. She could drive a golf ball 250 yards. Her drives did not necessarily go straight, and she might have sacrificed some distance for the sake of greater accuracy. But the Babe was an entertainer at heart, and if the people wanted to see her hit it long, she was not about to disappoint them. The Hepburn-Tracy movie *Pat and Mike* is loosely based on her career, and Zaharias—she was married to George Zaharias, a professional wrestler—makes a cameo appearance in it.

After the 1932 Olympics, Babe was declared a "professional" by the sports authorities and barred from competing in amateur events, golf included. But she was an extremely popular figure around the country, and she made do. Among other things, she toured with her own basketball team and barnstormed cross-country as the star attraction of a traveling baseball team. Some nights at the games she would entertain the crowds by fielding grounders or taking out her clubs and hitting long drives. At other times she played exhibitions with the touring golf pros, again showing off her long-hitting abilities.

The Babe had great flair and showmanship—qualities in short supply on today's tours, both men's and women's. After a round of golf she would take out her harmonica and entertain people in the clubhouse. She relished attention, loved an audience. And she was chock-full of confidence, the mark of a gifted athlete. Paired with Zaharias for an important four-ball match, Peggy Kirk Bell was jittery about it and said so. "Forget it," the Babe told her. "I can beat any two players in this tournament by myself. If I need any help, I'll let you know."

Zaharias was reinstated as an amateur in 1946 and proceeded to win seventeen tournaments in a row. She won the U.S. Women's Amateur and the British Ladies Championship, the first Yank to do so, and in 1947 she turned pro again. Two years later, with Patty Berg, Louise Suggs, Betty Jameson, and other leading women golfers of the time, she helped form the Ladies Professional Golf Association. An earlier attempt to start a women's pro tour had failed. The reason: no Babe. Whatever she did, wherever she went, she was the star, and her widespread appeal among both sexes helped bring attention to the other fine women golfers mainly laboring away in obscurity. As a pro, Zaharias dominated just as she had as an amateur, winning dozens of tournaments including the 1954 U.S. Women's Open by a prodigious twelve strokes. She died of cancer two years later, her place in golf and sports lore permanently secure.

"Sometimes I find myself leaning back in a chair thinking about Babe, and I have to smile," Patty Berg said some years ago. "With Babe there never was a dull moment. Her tremendous enthusiasm for golf and life was contagious. Even the galleries felt good when Babe was around."

The Natural

I try to feel oily.

—Sam Snead, when asked how he got ready
to hit a golf ball

You gotta like Sam Snead. You especially gotta like him if you think the game of golf is too gummed up with theories and analysis. "Thinking instead of acting is the number one golf disease," Snead said once. "If I'd become tangled up in the mechanics of the swing when I first hit shots, chances are I'd have only been an average golfer."

Too many golfers let themselves be overwhelmed by the thinking part of the game, but Snead was not one of them. His advice to golfers is refreshingly free of cant:

- On holding the club: "Hold it as you would a bird. Lightly—you mustn't hurt it."
- After watching a recreational golfer hit: "The only thing wrong with your swing is what's wrong with most amateurs. You don't hit the ball with your practice swing."
- On using the whole body: "When I play my best, I feel I'm playing with my legs and my feet."
- On the backswing: "Complete your backswing. That's the best advice you'll ever get, no matter your age. It's second only to 'Count your change.' The best way to complete your backswing is to give yourself time to do it."
- On rhythm and tempo: "When I got my first set of steel shafts, I'd end up hitting one five-iron one hundred and sixty yards and the next maybe two hundred and ten. That's when I started practicing rhythm. I've never worked on anything else since then. Rhythm—it's everything."
- There are, of course, some people who just don't get it. Snead, to a hacker: "You just have one problem. You stand too close to the ball—after you hit it." And his final piece of advice: "Lay off for three weeks and then quit for good."

Born and raised in the Back Creek Mountains of Virginia, Snead had one of the easiest and most graceful swings ever. People called him a natural—someone born to hit a golf club. "Watching Sam Snead hit practice balls is like watching a fish practice swimming," a writer once remarked. Bobby Jones was among the many who described Snead's unhurried swing as the best he'd ever seen. But for all his native gifts, Snead had to make choices just like every other golfer, had to sift through the numerous voices that go through a person's head as he's about to hit and decide which were worth listening to and which were not. Snead's genius was that he could ignore the rabble competing for attention in his head and heed the one voice he knew offered the best chance for success: his own.

Snead believed in trusting your own instincts on a golf course. This simple rule carried him to more wins on the PGA Tour than anyone else and despite never having won a U.S. Open, a long and fruitful golf-playing life. The story of how Snead took up golf is, by now, legend. As a boy he carved his clubs from the swamp-maple and hickory trees in the hills around his home, and he first practiced his swing using acorns. He would watch his brother Homer hit— golf balls, not acorns—in their backyard and copy him. Supposedly a muddy swamp lay on the right side of the Snead family pasture, and if young Samuel didn't want to lose his golf balls, he had to hit to the left rather than the right. This tendency stayed with him throughout his competitive career, as Snead preferred to hit a draw over a fade any day.

When he was in his forties, Snead wanted to see how well he could still handle a stick. So he conducted an experiment, cutting off a relatively straight swamp-maple branch with a bulge at the end like a golf club. Though he did some retooling on it, it was still basically a stick, plain and simple. Using that stick and a wedge, he went around a regulation course in 76. On a long par 5, hitting with the stick, he reached the green in two.

Stories like that about Snead abound. How he played a practice round at Augusta National in his bare feet and shot a 68. How he used to catch trout with his bare hands in the creek back home, and how, as an adult, he caught a ten-pound bass in a pond at Augusta (with a rod). How he played one-handed—his left hand—and shot in the eighties three days in a row, with a hole in one to boot. How he could hit three-hundred-yard drives straight. How he was so limber that he could kick an eight-foot-high ceiling with his foot. How he could bend forward, his legs stiff, and pick a ball out of the cup.

On top of his reputation as a great golfer, Snead was known as a bit of a country bumpkin as well. When told that Bing Crosby had won an Academy Award, Snead reportedly said, "That's great. Was it match or medal play?" In 1937, in the first year of Bing's famous tournament, Snead was presented with the winner's check of $500. "If you don't mind, Mr. Crosby, I'd rather have cash," he said. But Snead, as is usually the case with these country-bumpkin types, was a lot shrewder than he appeared. He found that being a good ole country boy from the backwoods of Virginia helped him pry loose the wallets of some of the Northern city slickers he played with. Snead, who professed to enjoy golf a little more when there was money on the line, was one of the game's most storied hustlers.

When Snead joined the tour in 1936, he was a strapping, rock-hard twenty-four-year-old who could, in his words, "run bears up and down ridges until they were ready to drop." The first event he entered was the Hershey Open in Pennsylvania, and all anyone knew about him was that he was from the South and kind of a hick. On the third round Snead's partner was Gene Sarazen, then still regarded as one of the game's best players. After watching Snead crush the ball all day long, Sarazen came back to the clubhouse exhausted. "I've just finished a round with a kid who doesn't know the first thing about playing golf," he said. "But I'll tell you something. I don't want to be around when he learns how." In a peculiar kind of way, Samuel Jackson Snead never did learn how to play golf, at least not the way the experts teach it, and that's what made him so good.

Ben Hogan and the Dream of Golf Perfection

Ben Hogan dreamed once that he was playing a round of golf and had made seventeen holes in one in a row. On each hole he would step up to the tee and knock the ball in with a single swing of his club. But on the eighteenth hole he watched as his ball rolled straight for the hole and slid tantalizingly off the edge of the cup. Hogan had missed the perfect round, and he woke up with a start.

To a person of a certain generation, Ben Hogan was the best. "Somebody asked me once, Who's better—Nicklaus or Hogan?" said Tommy Bolt. "Well, my answer was, I saw Nicklaus watch Hogan practice, but I never saw Hogan watch Nicklaus practice." The stoical, aptly named Iceman is widely regarded as one of the three greatest ever, along with Nicklaus and Bobby Jones. Not surprisingly, Nicklaus admired both Jones, whom he never saw play, and Hogan, whom he played against. "I grew up in the era of Hogan," Nicklaus recalled once. "Everything I saw of him and read of him and heard of him indicated that he had achieved utter mechanical perfection in the striking of a golf ball." The young Nicklaus sought to emulate many of Hogan's techniques, and in so doing the pupil may have surpassed his master.

The Hogan name is most familiar to golfers today as a manufacturer of equipment, as well as the new Ben Hogan Tour for young wanna-be's hoping to make it to the Big Show. Their picture of Hogan, the competitor, is understandably dim, as his greatest years on the tour were four decades ago. This lack of awareness may be at the root of the comment by David Graham, the 1981 U.S. Open winner, who said that "there are fifteen guys out there now who are better players than Ben Hogan ever was."

But it's foolish to get into a "Who's better?" debate. Hogan himself would certainly not have engaged in it, at least not on the golf course. Out there, he hardly talked at all. Talk distracted him from the game, and the game was everything to Ben. It's like the old joke: it wasn't a matter of life and death for him, it was more serious than that.

Hogan was the ultimate golfing perfectionist. Nobody practiced longer and worked at it harder than he did. He practiced until his hands hurt. When he got a carton of new golf balls, he would study each ball with a magnifying glass, now and then tossing one out. What's wrong with them? someone asked him. "Some of the dimples have too much paint in them," he replied. Filming a TV commercial for his golf company, Hogan was asked to hit some soft approach shots toward the pin. "Do you want the ball to come in from the right or the left?" he asked the cameraman. "And do you want it to back up?" In Hogan's mind, these were important questions. There was nothing frivolous about the act of striking a golf ball; it should be done correctly, or why do it at all?

True to his perfectionist bent, Hogan believed in intense preparation before a tournament. "The most important factor in playing a championship is to be fully prepared," he has said. Stories circulated around the tour that he would chart out his round on a blackboard in his motel each night before play. At Carnoustie, before his 1953 British Open win, he walked the course from back to front to memorize its topography. This was typical of the Hogan approach, which sought to minimize, if not eliminate, the role of luck or chance in the game. Championship golf, according to Hogan, was "twenty percent ability and eighty percent management." Unlike Arnold Palmer, the man who displaced him as the king of golf, Hogan was not a risk-taker. He figured that the best way to get out of trouble on a golf course was to avoid it in the first place. There's a funny story about how a tee shot of Palmer's rolled into a ditch behind a tree, one of those impossible situations he was always getting into. Spotting the sportswriter Jim Murray in the gallery, Palmer called out to him, "Well, you're always writing about Ben Hogan. What would Hogan do in a situation like this?" Said Murray: "Hogan wouldn't be in a situation like that."

Michael Murphy, the author and golf spiritualist, said that Hogan gave off "a tangible aura" on a golf course. "I remember someone at the 1955 U.S. Open remarking that nearly everyone who was watching him seemed subtly hypnotized," said Murphy. What hypnotized them was the precision and cold beauty of Hogan's shotmaking skills. Many have compared the experience of watching him to seeing a finely tuned, well-oiled machine at work. "Hogan's control of the ball was such that he seemed to allow it no option but to go where he wanted it to go," said an admiring sportswriter. Hogan had never played in Scotland before journeying to Carnoustie in 1953. But he adapted his game immediately to the different conditions and won the British Open convincingly, coming home with a last-day 68. "And if he had needed a 64 on his final round, you were quite certain he could have played a 64," wrote Bernard Darwin. "Hogan gave you the distinct impression that he was capable of getting whatever score he needed." That was the impression Hogan gave everybody, that he could do just about whatever he chose on a golf course.

Johnny Miller, like Nicklaus, studied the Hogan swing when he was young. He marveled that Hogan could move the ball a dozen different ways without changing his grip or swing. (Parenthetically, Miller's 63 at Oakmont in 1973 and Hogan's 67 at Oakland Hills in 1951 probably rank as the two finest finishing rounds in U.S. Open play.) His swing was not a "natural" one, like that of Sam Snead; it seemed to be constructed out of pieces, the way you would assemble the parts of a—yes, here it is again—machine. He gave new meaning to the term "sweet spot," and visitors to Golf House in Far Hills, New Jersey, can see his 1-iron with its well-worn, dime-sized groove where he unfailingly, time after time after time, stung that ball. Hogan, of course, invented the famous "pane of glass" image regarding the action of a golf swing, and his books, particularly *Five Lessons: The Modern Fundamentals of Golf* with Herbert Warren Wind, still have tremendous relevance today. Hogan was so respected as a teacher that Gary Player once sought him out for advice well after Ben had retired from the circuit. Hoping to get a tip or two over the phone, Player, calling from South Africa, reached Hogan in the Fort Worth office of his golf manufacturing company. "And whose clubs do you use?" Hogan asked Player after listening to his question. "Why, Dunlop," responded Player. "Then go get a lesson from Mr. Dunlop," Ben said, and hung up.

Hogan, a Fort Worth native, never won any Mr. Congeniality awards from his fellow pros. Irascible at turns, a loner by nature, he had no time for idle chitchat when engaged in the serious business of golf. "About all Ben ever said in a tournament," said Sam Snead, "was 'Good luck' on the first tee and 'You're away' a few times after that." At the 1954 Masters he was paired with Byron Nelson, who had retired from tournament golf years earlier and was playing as the sentimental guest of Augusta National. "That's a beauty," Lord Byron said after a Hogan drive, and then again after another Hogan shot: "That's a beauty, Ben." Yet not once during the entire round did Hogan acknowledge the compliments with so much as a smile or a nod of the head. Which was probably just as well, because Hogan could bite your head off if you talked too much around him, even if the talk was flattering. After a fellow pro complimented him on a shot, Hogan snapped, "I wish you wouldn't say that. I'm the only one who knows how I wanted to hit that shot."

Hogan was paired with Claude Harmon during the 1947 Masters when Harmon, hitting first, nailed an ace on the famous 12th. This was the first-ever hole in one on that absurdly difficult, 155-yard par 3. The crowd went wild when it saw the ball roll into the hole, but Hogan remained mute. Did not crack a smile or say a word to his overjoyed partner. Stepping up for his own shot, he hit an excellent ball that landed only a few feet from the cup.

When the twosome arrived at the green, the gallery greeted the well-liked Harmon with more cheers and applause. Still, the Iceman said nothing, concentrating on his own putt, which he dropped for a birdie. Finally, as the pair approached the next tee, Hogan broke his silence. "You know, Claude," he said, "that's the first two I've ever made on that hole."

For all of his lack of emotion on a golf course, the Hogan legend also includes a highly emotional comeback from a car accident that nearly cost him his life. In February 1949, a bus crashed into him and his wife, Valerie, while they were driving home to Fort Worth from a tournament in Arizona. Hogan suffered multiple fractures of his pelvis, collarbone, ribs, and ankle, and an ambulance rushed him to the hospital for emergency surgery. On the operating table Ben cried out, "Back on the left! Back on the left!" as if, in his delirium, he was talking to a gallery that was crowding him. But it was not a surprise to his fellow pros that Hogan recovered from his injuries and rejoined the tour; they expected nothing less of him. The year after the accident, at the 1950 U.S. Open, Hogan won in a playoff though his legs were bandaged and he could not bend low enough to pick the ball from the cup.

Hogan's greatest year was 1953, when, at age forty-one, the grim-visaged, white-capped automaton took the British and U.S. Opens and the Masters, setting a scoring record at Augusta. But the high point of his career must be two years before that, at the 1951 Open at Oakland Hills, Michigan. Playing on one of the toughest Open courses ever—a souped-up, high-rough, narrow-track torture pit masterminded by Robert Trent Jones—only two players, Hogan and Clayton Heafner, broke 70 on any round. Hogan's rounds at Oakland Hills possessed an almost mathematical beauty: 76, 73, 71, 67. Each round he understood more about the course, each round he got better. At the awards ceremony after his 67, he said, "I am glad I brought this course, this monster, to its knees," which, for a man of so few words, was one of the most memorable things anyone has ever said after an Open. Others in the tournament—those whom the Monster had tamed—were awestruck by Hogan's performance. "Hogan must be playing a different course than the rest of us," said Bobby Locke. Claude Harmon was more jocular: "Ben," he said to him, "if you keep playing like this, every player is going to go out and get hit by a bus."

Nevertheless, the man was never satisfied. As long as he played, he was never satisfied. Even in his seventies, while working at his Fort Worth company, Hogan would go out during lunch and hit balls at a nearby country club. But he wouldn't let people watch him as he practiced; pride would not allow that. So he would go out by himself to a remote part of the course where no one could see him. The ostensible purpose for his solitary play was to test the new clubs and balls that his company was developing, but it's intriguing to speculate about another possible reason. After all the golf he had played in his life, after the years and years of tournaments and the endless hours of practice, Hogan, an old man still consumed by a dream, may have been out there just trying to get it . . . *right*.

The Limited Virtues of Practice

Ben Hogan was a great believer in practice. "Every day you don't hit balls is one day longer it takes you to get better," he said. Before Hogan, few of the leading golfers bothered to practice, and certainly none did with the zeal of the Iceman. Nowadays, of course, with all the riches at stake on the pro tours, the Hogan work ethic is universally accepted. Even among recreational golfers, those who play for "fun," the three p's—practice, practice, practice—are considered the cornerstone for improving your game. Go to any driving range in America and you will find these industrious, sober-faced, sweaty-palmed men and women dutifully beating balls into the darkness and beyond, if the range is lit. All this hard work is no doubt paying off for them, on the driving range if not on the golf course, but one should keep in mind that practice can only take you so far, and in the case of Carl Lohren, it will get you nowhere.

Lohren was a touring pro so sold on improving his golf game that if he was riding in a car with somebody, he'd jump out at red lights and practice his swing. Traveling the South to go to a tournament in Florida, Lohren did his jump-out-and-groove-that-swing routine as the car he was riding in stopped at a railroad crossing to let a train pass. But his buddy behind the wheel thought Lohren was in the backseat sleeping and didn't see him hop out of their convertible. After the train went by, the car started up again, leaving Lohren standing in the middle of nowhere with a well-oiled swing but without his suitcase, his money, or his clubs. It's not known whether Lohren ever made it to the tournament.

How to Putt

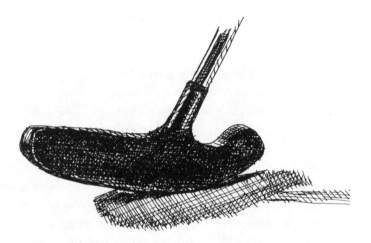

He does his best, but oh! that horrid lip!
The curling ball disdains the trifling dip.

—Poem, circa 1895

How do you sink a putt? Don't ask the experts. They don't know any better than you or me. "I think I know as well as anybody how not to do it," said Harry Vardon, a wonder with the irons but a clunker with the putter. A player of more recent vintage—Bob Charles, a lefty—thinks that you can throw out everything you read in those how-to manuals. "Method or technique is less than five percent of putting," he says. The New Zealander may not have put much stock in method, but he was a stickler in making sure his balls were just so. Before playing he would sort through a box of new balls, throwing out any that were not perfectly spherical or did not suit his specifications in some other way. Charles rejected ten of every twelve balls he saw.

Bobby Locke was one of the best putters ever. A South African, he won a handful of British Opens and a bunch of dough on the U.S. tour by finessing his way around the greens with an old hickory-shafted putter given to him as a boy. Locke coddled that putter as if it were his lover. He never let it spend the night in his golf bag; when he was on the road, it stayed with him in his hotel room. Locke, like Charles and all the good putters, was a believer in the power of positive thinking. "Make up your mind what you are going to do, then go ahead and do it," said Bobby.

Go ahead, then! Stand up there and knock that sucker in! And if it doesn't work, do what George Low used to do: *kick it*. Low could putt better with his foot than most people can with a superbly balanced Slot-Line. The skill won him a hefty shoe-endorsement contract, in fact.

"There are very few truths in putting," Arnold Palmer said. "You get the ball in the hole, and it doesn't matter how." Palmer was an exceptional putter in his prime. He had a forceful, assertive approach; he "willed" the ball into the hole, they said. "Don't hope, don't try, and don't second-guess your vision of line and speed," he also said. But like anyone else, Palmer fell into bouts of second-guessing. When that occurred, he was not above spending an afternoon sinking one-foot putts into that 4½-inch-diameter hole just to restore his battered confidence.

Nicklaus, too, was a compulsive fidgeter with his putting, changing some aspect of his style two or three times in the course of a four-day tournament. Others have been equally inventive. There is the case of the 1970s-era West Coast amateur who putted from behind his back. Gripping the club behind him, he would stick his putter between his legs and stroke the ball. Hey, if it works, why not?

The old-timers could be equally inventive. Olin Dutra, winner of the 1934 U.S. Open, possessed "an arms akimbo putting style that gave him the appearance of an octopus that had lost most of its tentacles," according to Bob Drum. Chick Evans thought it was less a matter of style and more of equipment. He carried four putters in his bag. He would miss, pick out a new putter, miss again, pick out another putter, miss again, and so on until he made the damn thing or ran out of putters. The USGA frowns on such highjinks now, nor does it allow you to putt with a pool cue. A Richard Peters tried to do that in an early U.S. Amateur and quickly got shown the exit.

Many people experiment with their grip. Some older players, beset by the cursed yips, use the extra-long putter developed by Charles Owens. Some try a heavier club, or hitting one-handed. The elder Sam Snead tried a croquet-style approach; after the golfing authorities banned it, he went to a side-straddle approach that made him the butt of jokes. Snead's response: "When you come in off the course, they don't ask you how. They ask you how many." Norman von Nida, the Australian, got so fed up with his putting that for a time he junked his putter altogether and used a 2-iron on the greens.

Dave Marr heard voices when he putted. On the 16th green at the 1965 PGA, he claimed he heard his baby say, "Daddy, be careful!" as he lined up his putt. On the 17th, with Nicklaus thundering into contention behind him, Marr heard a deeper, sterner voice: "Damnit. Don't let him in, just lock the guy out." Marr listened to this last voice and went on to win by two strokes.

Ben Hogan, ever the perfectionist, could not perfect his putting. His putting cost him many a tournament, the more so as he got older, and he once advocated picking up after a golfer reached the green and just adding two strokes to his total for the hole. Roberto de Vicenzo, the poor fellow who signed an incorrect scorecard and lost a Masters, would change putters every week. He bought a new putter every time he went into a pro shop, and his closet was full of his discards. Roberto finally found a mallet putter that he liked, but he knew that nothing was forever when it came to the game on the greens. "The putt is a funny game," said the native Argentinian. "You can't think you got it for always. You can lose it tomorrow."

If you do lose it tomorrow, you might try doing what Arthur Lee, a former British Ryder Cupper, did. After missing a long putt he asked his caddie to retrieve the ball for him. "Just as I thought," he said as he rolled it around in his fingers, "I knew the bugger wasn't round," and he tossed the ball into the bushes. Another possible approach might be to give your putter a name, as you would your dog or cat. Bobby Jones was terrific on the greens; his putter, the most famous of all putters, was named Calamity Jane. Willie Park, a nineteenth-century great, named his putter Old Pawky. "The man who can putt is a match for anyone," Willie said, and with Old Pawky at his side, he was. As a youngster Park practiced putting on the brick floor of his Scottish home. It's not hard to believe Willie when he said he never faced a putting surface as tricky as that old brick floor.

Not to be overlooked is Little Ben, the putting stick of Ben Crenshaw, who's acknowledged as one of the very best putters in the world today. Like Bobby Locke, Crenshaw has cultivated a long-term relationship with his prized putter, playing with Little Ben for more than twenty years. It was given to him when he was a boy, and he has since parlayed it into a Masters title and a country estate in Texas. A couple of years ago Little Ben was lost—or more likely, stolen—at the Atlanta airport, and its owner was devastated, offering a $2,000 reward to anyone who could supply information leading to its recovery. The putter apparently changed hands a few times—is there a black market for good putters?—before a golfer recognized it and returned it to its rightful owner.

Less than two months later Ben and Little Ben went on a rampage at the Colonial Open in Fort Worth, whipping through the front nine on the last day in 30 and finishing with an overall 66. On that final eighteen Crenshaw made every putt under fifteen feet, and four of his birdie putts were between fifteen and thirty feet. Two par-saving putts on the back nine were of six and twelve feet. Now, when Crenshaw comes to an airport, he lets the airline attendants know what his priorities are. "I tell them, 'This is Katherine, my two-year-old daughter, and this' "—here, he holds up his esteemed companion—" 'this is Little Ben.' "

The Fine Art
of Throwing a Golf Club

Golf is a game that creates emotions that sometimes cannot be sustained with the club still in one's hand.

—*Bob Jones*

In the early years of tournament golf, there were plenty of hot-blooded golfers who would just as soon throw a club as look at it. The great Mr. Jones, for one, was a veritable Vesuvius of golf when he was a youngster. His golf-course eruptions featured a number of impressive displays of club-throwing prowess. "It's gone forever, an irrevocable crime," he said once, describing how it felt to make a bad shot, "and when you feel a fool, and a bad golfer to boot, what can you do except to throw the club away?"

Well put, Bob. But unfortunately for connoisseurs of the art, the young Jones eventually matured into a more sober adulthood and abandoned the practice. This loss, however, was more than made up for by the many other tempestuous club flingers who, thankfully, did not follow the Jones example.

Ky Laffoon used to get so mad at his putter that he'd attach a string to it, stick it out the window of his car, and drag it along the road as he drove. That was when he wasn't dunking it into a lake and screeching, "Drown, sucker! Drown!" If someone inquired as to what Laffoon was doing during one of these moments, he'd reply that it was a matter between him and his putter so butt out. But Laffoon's fury was not reserved solely for his putter. He could get plenty peeved at his other clubs, too. It was not unheard of for Laffoon to get so frustrated as he was playing that he would start jettisoning clubs during the course of a round. Damn driver! To hell with you, 7-iron! And out they would go—into a pond or a ditch or wherever. By the 15th or 16th hole Laffoon wouldn't have any clubs left, and he'd be playing out of his partner's bag.

Lefty Stackhouse could match Laffoon as a club-destroyer, adding some nice touches in the self-abuse department as well. After hitting a bad shot he would kick himself in the shin or smack his hand against a tree. "Take that," he'd tell his bloodied hand. "That'll teach you." After a round of 80 he once hurled himself bodily into some rose bushes and flailed away at himself in anger. He was known to break every club in his bag after a bad round, club by club. Then, for good measure, he'd tear apart his bag.

You always knew Lefty was nearby because you could hear him on the next fairway, swearing at the top of his lungs. He'd swear at his driver before he used it, telling it that it had better behave or else. It was the same with the ball. But his ball and clubs must not have been listening because they kept having to take the punishment Lefty meted out. Lefty once destroyed his car radiator by beating it to death with his putter (poor putters, they get all the abuse). Give him credit, though. He found some very creative ways to exact revenge. After one particularly poor outing Lefty blew his stack completely and set fire to his clubs. This was in the days of wood-shafted golf clubs, which made for terrific kindling. One can almost picture Lefty rubbing his hands with satanic glee, his eyes bright with mischief and insane joy, as his clubs were consumed by the fire.

Ivan Gantz was yet another of the nearly forgotten individuals who have made impressive contributions to the club-throwing art. Ivan the Terrible was known to bop himself in the head with his putter when a putt didn't go in. He would keep right on playing, blood streaming down his forehead. Ivan was such a wild man he would throw himself facedown into a bunker or a creek after a bad shot. Or he might hurl himself onto the middle of a fairway and roll in the grass pummeling himself wildly. Then, if his putter wasn't handy, he might bloody his forehead with a rock. Ivan could blow up at any time and even threw clubs during practice.

Clayton Heafner, who played in the forties and fifties, had a fiery personality, too. He was one of those guys who seem to walk around with a perpetual chip on his shoulder. He threw a few clubs in his time, but his anger revealed itself even before he reached the golf course. In the old days of the tour the pros had to drive from tournament to tournament. Heafner would jump in his car—he was a hard driver—and he'd drive and drive and while he was out on that long, lonesome highway, he'd have lots of time to think. And he'd start thinking about the golf course where he was going. He'd think about it and think about it, and he'd get so mad thinking about all the mean, rotten, nasty things that could happen to him on that golf course that when he finally arrived, he'd pull up to the clubhouse, poke his head in the front door, and yell, "Your course is a goddamned pasture!" and then turn around and drive away.

The Dandy

When I get out on that green carpet called a
fairway and manage to poke the ball right down the middle,
my surroundings look like heaven on earth.

—*Jimmy Demaret*

Jimmy Demaret was as dandy a golfer as he was a dresser. He won three Masters titles, and no less an authority than Ben Hogan described him as the finest shotmaker he'd ever seen (out of modesty, Hogan had to discount himself). But Sunny Jim—so dubbed for his upbeat disposition—did not share Hogan's monastic approach to the game. Unlike Hogan, he never practiced. For him tournament golf was a show, and when you're in show business, you must first of all look the part. "If you're going to be in the limelight," said Demaret, "you might as well dress for it."

Indeed, he did. He wore hot-pink shoes and polka-dot slacks. He was showy as a peacock, dressing in slacks-and-jacket combinations of fire-engine red, lemon yellow, luscious lavender, and whatever else suited his fancy. If neon clothing had been around then, he would have worn that, too. He was into imported pastels long before Don Johnson and "Miami Vice." Over his playing career, which spanned the late thirties, forties, and fifties, it was said that he owned five hundred hats. By the midfifties, in addition to his headgear, he owned seventy pairs of slacks, twenty sweaters, six dozen shirts, and forty of those garish sport coats.

Demaret was one of the good guys of golf. Fun to be around, quick-witted, charming with the ladies. He was a partyer, and some-times when you were out with Sunny Jim night turned to day and the 19th hole went on to become the 20th and 21st holes. He was known to close down bars—besides his many other talents, he was a professional singer—and then tee off in a tournament the next day. Demaret, said sportswriter Blackie Sherrod, a fellow Texan, "could sing all night and shoot sixty-four by dawn's early light." Critics said that his after-hours life hurt his golf, but Demaret—who once shot a 30 on the back nine at Augusta—shrugged them off. "If I didn't have such a good time playing golf, I don't think I'd play as well as I do," he said once.

The Houston-born Demaret joined the tour in 1935, throwing his clubs into the trunk of his car and heading west for the Los Angeles Open. On the way he made a side trip to Juárez, Mexico, and gambled away the car, the clubs, and $600 he had borrowed from some Texas backers. He sent the pawn ticket for the clubs to his brother back home in Houston and rode a freight train to the Coast. Legend has it that he lived on sandwiches and cheap wine until he could get some sticks and start making money again.

It was only a matter of time before a man of Demaret's sensibilities struck up with the golf-playing Hollywood set, and he became fast friends with Bing Crosby, Phil Harris, and others who did not mind mixing their golf with a wee bit of late-night merriment. One of the things that made Demaret such an attractive personality was a fresh, lively wit, examples of which abound:

Paired one year with Bob Hope at the Crosby tournament, Hope hooked his tee shot out-of-bounds on the first hole. "Don't worry," said Demaret. "There's always next year."

Demaret once said of Hope's game: "Bob has a great short game. Unfortunately, it's off the tee." On another occasion at Pebble Beach, Hope's ball had come to rest on the fairway. "Can I get home from here?" the comedian asked. "I don't know," replied Demaret. "Where do you live?"

Demaret can claim some of the most famous one-liners in golf lore. After Arnold Palmer took a 9 on the 17th at Pebble, driving over the green and landing in the rocks along the edge of the Pacific Ocean, someone asked why Arnie hadn't taken a drop as a way out of his difficulty. "Because from where he was," said Demaret, "his closest drop was Honolulu."

Demaret made the definitive comment on the elder Sam Snead's side-straddle putting style—"He looks like he's basting a turkey"—and when asked which touring pro had the most even disposition, he replied: "Clayton Heafner. He's mad *all* the time." There's his classic line about Tommy Bolt and his club-throwing fits of anger: "Tommy Bolt's putter has spent more time in the air than Lindbergh." Less well known, but equally sharp, is the one about the fellow taking too long to line up his putt: "He's not only studying the grain—he's reading the roots."

Demaret served as a host, with Gene Sarazen, on "Shell's Wonderful World of Golf" TV series in the fifties and acted as a commentator for both radio and television. It may not have been his wittiest moment, but his remark at the 1953 World Championships of Golf in Chicago set a standard for candor that all broadcasters should try to emulate. After Lew Worsham knocked in an impossible eagle two to steal the event on the last hole, Demaret, who was interviewing the anticipated winner at the time, blurted out over the air: "The son of a bitch went in!"

A Fine and Noble Tradition

〜〜〜

Drinking has a long and glorious tradition in golf. One of the game's most persistent legends pertains to drinking—that the Scots chose eighteen holes because there were eighteen nips in a bottle, one nip for each hole. One wag jokes that the Scots settled on eighteen because after they started drinking, they couldn't count any higher. Neither story is true, but they do make for good yuks while sitting around your local 19th-hole establishment, which is, after all, one of the immutable pleasures of the game.

Lang Willie would testify to that. Willie was a St. Andrews caddie of long ago, and a man who liked his liquor. After a day of toting the sticks around for some out-of-town tourist, Lang Willie, who was six feet six inches tall and wore a stovepipe hat à la Abraham Lincoln, would frequently retire to the pub and have a pint or three. Some days Willie might start a little earlier than usual—say, around breakfasttime—and so it was that one of the stuffier members of the Royal and Ancient accused him of being drunk on the course. "Ay, that I am," returned Lang Willie with a stare that would melt wax. "But I'll get sober. There ain't nothin' you can do about that golf game of yours."

Golfers have never been teetotalers. In the middle 1700s, Tobias Smollett, the Scottish-born novelist, observed a golf match in Leith and wrote this account of what he saw: "Hard by, in the field called the Links, the citizens of Edinburgh divert themselves at a game called golf. Of this diversion the Scotch are so fond that, when the weather will permit, you may see a multitude of all ranks mingled together in their shirts, and following the ball with the utmost eagerness." Of particular fascination for Smollett was a group of men golfers in their eighties: "They were all gentlemen of independent fortunes, who had amused themselves with this pastime for the best part of a century, without ever having felt the least alarm for sickness or disgust; and they never went to bed without having each the best part of a gallon of claret in his belly. Such uninterrupted exercise, cooperating with the keen air of the seas, must, without doubt, keep the appetite always on edge, and steel the constitution against all the common attacks of distemper."

A daily round of eighteen, fresh air, and wine—now *there's* the key to a long and happy life. One time a band of Edinburgh golfers finished off their day on the links with a party at a local hotel. As the evening wore on, the party got louder and louder until a waiter knocked on their door and asked the men to quiet down. The rowdy golfers promptly threw the waiter out the window of their room and resumed their drinking. In time, though, the liquor ran low and they hollered for someone to bring more. "You'll just have to be patient," the hotel proprietor said when he appeared at their door. "You killed the waiter who was helping you before."

"Too bad!" shouted one of the men. "Just put him on the bill and send us another!"

When golfers of old got together at the pub, it was not uncommon for them to raise their mugs in song, such as this one about the women they left behind:

But the young golf widows, O my brothers,
They are weeping bitterly,
They are weeping in the playtime of the others,
While you're swiping from the tee.

To "swipe" meant to drive in those days, but a duffer will always be a duffer:

See yonder lads upon the links,
Go, find a duffer there but thinks
For a' the jeers and wylie winks,
He'll yet a gowfer be!

The early British golf clubs—indeed, virtually all of the world's most venerable golf clubs—were essentially formed as men's drinking societies. They ate, they drank, and if they were up to it, they played a spot of golf. "It is apparent that the members played hard, drank hard, and had a roaring, rollicking good time playing their favorite game," writes Herb Graffis. Graffis, until his death a longtime observer of the golf scene, tells the story of a new member wandering through the tradition-soaked clubhouse of Augusta National one winter evening. "Where are all the golfers?" he asked a waiter. "I didn't see many while we were playing this afternoon."

"They'll be here," said the waiter. "Right now, this is mainly a drinking club."

A round of golf is hardly complete until you've had a beverage of some sort to help you relive—or forget, as the case may be— any or all of those eighteen holes. That's true today, and that was true in the days of Harry Vardon, the great turn-of-the-century English golfer. Back then if a golfer had bellied up to the bar and ordered a Perrier with a twist of lemon, he would've been thrown out on his ear. Vardon was on one of his exhibition tours of the United States when he was beseeched by a woman to swear off drinking. "Moderation is essential in all things, madam," said Harry, "but never in my life have I been beaten by a teetotaler."

Another noted imbiber from yesteryear, Tommy Armour, was asked why he never drank water on a golf course. "Fish fornicate in water," he said.

Unlike Vardon or Armour, the players on the current PGA Tour are mainly a bunch of teetotalers, and so it is left to those of us in the amateur ranks to carry on this fine and noble tradition. But even among the sobersided pros, there are occasional exceptions. At the 1990 Irish Open in Portmarnock, a Swedish golfer, Mikael Krantz, showed up to play after attending a party the night before with some Irish friends and getting steamrollered by Guinness Stout. Come morning Krantz was still drunk. He managed to get to the first tee all right, but after hitting his drive he fell flat on his face, pulling his caddie and a tournament official down to the ground with him. He hit his next shot into Dublin Bay and carded an 83, not a bad score considering his condition. Afterward the chastened Krantz promised tournament officials that he would never again try to play golf after attending a party where Guinness was being served.

Average Golfer, Great Drinker

Phil Harris was an average golfer but a terrific drinker. He deserves at least a footnote in any chronicle of drinking and the royal and ancient game. Harris was the bandleader-turned-comedian who acted as "social director" of the Crosby Pro-Am at Pebble Beach for so many years. He was a pal of Bing's and a Hollywood star who helped establish the Clambake's reputation in the fifties and sixties as one of the wettest stops on the PGA Tour (in an alcohol sense, although it applied to the weather, too).

Harris had nearly as many gag lines about golf as Bob Hope. "My golf game is so bad I'm having my retriever regripped," he joked once. Plagued by a chronic slice, he said he finally found a cure: "I quit playing." But at the 1951 Crosby, Harris teamed with the pro Dutch Harrison to win the pro-am side of the tournament after Phil sank a long, long putt on the 17th green at Pebble Beach. Asked how far the putt traveled, Harris cracked, "I don't know, but I'd love to own that much footage on Wilshire Boulevard."

Harris's chief reputation, though, was as a boozer extraordinaire. "I've seen Phil send a ball two hundred and twenty-five yards—just by breathing on it," remarked his friend Bob Hope, who added that Harris was once five up on Dean Martin—"and that was before they left the bar." Martin and Harris were paired together one year when Harris, suffering mightily from a hangover, stepped up to the tee and whiffed. After stepping back to regroup, he moved forward and whiffed again on his second try. "Don't stop now," said Dean. "You've got a no-hitter going."

The best Harris story teams him up with his good friend Bing Crosby. One year the twosome made a pilgrimage to Scotland to play the old courses and get away from Hollywood for a while. While driving one night in the countryside, they saw the lights of a distillery twinkling in the distance.

"Look, Phil," said Bing. "They're making it faster than you can drink it."

"Yeah, but at least I got the bastards working nights," said Phil.

Lightning in a Bottle

Jimmy Demaret called it "lightning in a bottle," but it had nothing to do with what Phil Harris saw at the bottom of his Scotch glass. The lightning was supplied, in this case, by Jack Fleck, a municipal golf pro from Iowa who beat Ben Hogan in the 1955 U.S. Open to lay claim to the greatest golf upset of all time. Only the saga of how Sir Francis of Brookline slew the two-headed English dragon, the evil Vardon-Ray, rivals it for storybook power and drama.

The marvelous thing about the Fleck-Hogan face-off was the way it punctured expectations, not the least of which was Ben's himself. Hogan, the best of his time. The master technician, the shotmaker supreme. He was so confident he had won his fifth Open title that after walking off the 72nd green at the Olympic Club in San Francisco, he flipped his ball to Joe Dey, the head of the United States Golf Association. "Here, Joe," he said, "this is for Golf House," indicating that this was a golf ball for the ages and as such should be enshrined with the other mementos of the game's past.

It was not only Hogan who was fooled. Gene Sarazen, commenting on television, conceded the event to the Iceman—his fifth Open win in eight years. Hogan's 287 was unassailable; none of the other contenders could touch it. Sure, this Fleck guy was still out on the course, but who was he? A nobody. Nobodies don't beat Ben Hogan, not at the U.S. Open anyway. NBC-TV went off the air; the tournament was over, in its eyes. Relaxing over a Scotch and water in the clubhouse, the King was asked about the possibility of Fleck's catching him. He flicked the thought away like a man brushing a piece of lint off his lapel. "Good luck to him," Hogan said magnanimously.

But Fleck birdied two of the last four holes, including the 18th, and forced a playoff. The next day the two men again went out and stared each other down, and to the continuing surprise of the experts, it wasn't Fleck who blinked.

Fleck, the unlikely upstart, was thirty-two years old, ten years younger than his far more famous counterpart. Hogan and Fleck, Fleck and Hogan—the two shall always be linked together in golf, twins of fate. Fleck lived in Davenport, Iowa, and was an ex-Navy man. Growing up on a farm, he started in golf as a caddie, learning the game for himself by playing on Mondays on the Davenport course, the day they let the caddies play. In 1954, the year before the Open, he worked as both head pro and manager of Davenport's two muni courses. But he figured he could do better than that, and while his wife stayed home to take care of the shops, he tried his luck on the tour. Tall and lanky and long off the tee, Fleck made a little money, but nothing he had ever done on a golf course gave anyone even the slightest hint that he was capable of beating the greatest golfer in the world in the greatest tournament.

On the 3rd hole of the 18-hole playoff a rabbit ran across the green that the golfers were aiming for. "What I like to remember is the little gray rabbit that hopped across the green just before we hit," said Fleck, recalling how someone in the gallery wondered out loud whose luck that was. After the rabbit disappeared, Hogan drilled a classic 2-iron straight at the flag. Fleck's shot landed in a bunker and hippety-hopped out of the sand onto the green. Both men got pars, but a message was sent: the luck belonged to Fleck.

Hogan's loss to Fleck did not diminish his stature; in fact it may have enhanced it. For what truly distinguished the fallen champion was the way he carried himself in defeat. On the 6th hole of the playoff Fleck lay twenty-five feet from the cup. He was one stroke up, but he had hit two poor shots in a row and seemed frazzled, perhaps ready to crack. Hogan, meanwhile, was within birdie range.

"I'll be out of your way in a minute," said the harried Fleck.

"Take your time, Jack," Ben replied. "We have nowhere to go."

Hogan missed his birdie, and Fleck salvaged par with a long-range hallelujah putt. He then made birdies on 8, 9, and 10, carrying the lucky rabbit with him all the way to the end.

Hogan arrived at the 343-yard, par-4 18th only down a stroke, but his foot slipped on his tee shot and the ball bounded into heavy rough. It was all over. Fleck parred, Hogan double-bogeyed. Fleck got a 69, Hogan a 72. The King was dead.

"Maybe it would've been better if Ben had won," Fleck has said.

"That fifth Open meant a lot to him." It sure did. And there's a final irony: Fleck did all his sharpshooting using Ben Hogan–brand golf clubs. Earlier in the tournament, before lightning struck, a reporter had asked Hogan what he thought of Fleck as a golfer. "He must be a good player," the great man had said, and smiled. "He uses Hogan clubs."

Moments in the Sun

In golf, the dream is kept alive not by the Hogans and the Palmers and the Tom Watsons, but by the Jack Flecks and Mike Donalds and Billy Joe Pattons. They're the middle- or back-of-the-pack guys who, for one tournament, or one round in a tournament, suddenly tear off their spectacles, rip open their shirts, and reveal a big red "S" on their chests. That they inevitably revert, in a day or two, to their normal Clark Kent selves does not lessen their accomplishments at all.

Jack Fleck is the most conspicuous example of a golf overachiever, but there are many, many more. Johnny Goodman beat Bobby Jones in the 1929 U.S. Amateur, held that year in Pebble Beach. Goodman

121

hitched a ride to California from Nebraska on a freight train. Although he did not win the tournament, his defeat of the best golfer in the world was a shocking upset. Even more shocking would have been Billy Joe Patton's win at the 1954 Masters if the country boy from Morganton, North Carolina, had been able to pull it off. Billy Joe was leading the pack as late as the 13th hole on the final day. His two closest competitors were Sam Snead and Ben Hogan, and they were as astonished as everyone else that an amateur had a clear shot at beating them and walking off with the green coat.

If the galleries could have voted, it would have been a landslide for the talkative and likable Billy Joe, who was as loose and carefree as if he were playing a two-dollar Nassau at the local muni. "I may go for it, and I may not," he would say as he addressed his ball. "It all depends on what I elect to do on my backswing." But he elected wrong on 13, going for the green on his second shot instead of laying up and playing it safe. His ball landed in the drink and he took a seven. Two holes later he found water again and bogeyed. He missed the Snead-Hogan playoff by a stroke.

The history of golf sparkles with Rocky-esque figures who shouldn't have, but did. And if they didn't, they at least came far closer than any of the experts gave them a chance to. Mike Donald was a kind of nineties version of Billy Joe Patton, though with far less color. What characterized Donald, actually, was a lack of color. Well liked by his fellow pros, he was a thirty-four-year-old journeyman player who had won only one tournament in eleven years on the tour. But dreams die hard, and Donald, a bachelor who had given over his adult life to the pursuit of a mediocre career, dreamed of someday joining the ranks of Tony Manero, Orville Moody, Bob Tway, Larry Mize, Scott Simpson, and other unknowns who had won major championships.

And he almost did. After playing seventy-two holes at the U.S. Open at Medinah in 1990, he was tied with Hale Irwin. After eighteen playoff holes, he was still tied. But after one sudden-death hole, he was no longer tied and Irwin was the winner. "God bless him, I almost wish he had won," said Irwin about the heartbroken golfer who had finished second. "He's a great guy."

Another type of golf overachiever is the "rabbit," a person who startles everyone, most of all himself, by jumping into the lead of a tournament after the first day. Rabbits are often club pros or amateurs, and they're almost always well out of sight by Sunday when the real golf gets going. Nonetheless, they do some pretty nifty things during their short time in the spotlight.

Lee Mackey, a twenty-six-year-old Alabama native, shot a 64 at the opening round of the 1950 U.S. Open at Merion Golf Club in Pennsylvania. His then-record for eighteen holes at an Open included seven birdies and one bogey. The next day he skied to an 81, complaining, "Yesterday I couldn't get off the fairway and today I couldn't get on." This is typical of the rabbit species. Down today, up in a big way tomorrow. Bob Gajda, a forty-six-year-old club pro who had missed the cut in eight of the nine Opens he had played, shot a 69 on a tough Brookline, Massachusetts, course to take the first-round lead at the 1963 Open. As he was being led into the press room after his round, Jack Nicklaus was on his way out. "You shot a sixty-nine on that course?" said Nicklaus, obviously impressed. Gajda returned to reality the next three days with rounds in the 80s, but he can carry that compliment from Nicklaus to his grave.

Rabbits do not figure large in the scroll of golfing history, but they do make for great trivia questions down in small type at the bottom of the page. Who was the only player to break par in the first round of the 1961 U.S. Open? The answer: Bobby Brue, with a 69. Conscious of the tendency of rabbits to shoot in the stratosphere the day after their big round, Brue stayed steady and solid with a 72 and a 73 the next two days, although he did finish with a 78. "I was nervous," he said about his final round, "and all I could see was bunkers." Brue, a club pro from Milwaukee who now plays on the Senior Tour, was a headline writer's delight. After his opening 69, the headline in the papers read: "The Brue That Made Milwaukee Famous."

One of the more admirable qualities of rabbits is their lack of pretentiousness. They don't have the swell heads of the big stars, nor should they. At the U.S. Senior Open a few years ago, one J. Frank Boydston, the owner of two Chuckbox hamburger restaurants in the Phoenix area and a three handicapper, was among the first-round leaders. Playing with clubs he had bought at a flea market, Boydston shot a 69 and charmed the assembled media. "I'm pretty much a frustrated player with dreams of grandeur," he told them. "I just hope nobody pinches me and wakes me up." Asked his greatest strength as a golfer, Boydston answered, "My biggest asset is that when I miss the ball, it usually goes fairly straight." He added that it took him a long time to choose which club to play because they were so old and worn he couldn't read the numbers on them. J. Frank's scores went up over the next three days, and he finished in a tie for thirty-ninth for the tournament.

When the underdog wins in golf, just as in other sports, it's a victory for everybody. It turns the tables on accepted wisdom, confounds the experts, and gives bald men hope. In the early 1970s, Bobby Mitchell, an unheralded and little-known pro, beat the great Nicklaus in a playoff to win the Tournament of Champions at La Costa. To celebrate his triumph, the balding Mitchell went out and bought a toupee. If I can sink a twenty-foot birdie putt in sudden death to beat Jack Nicklaus, reasoned Mitchell, I can have hair.

A few weeks later he ran into Nicklaus at a party, the first time they'd seen each other since the tournament. Nicklaus was amazed, and almost didn't recognize the man who had beaten him.

"I knew it was a good win for you, Bobby," Jack said. "But how did it grow hair on your head?"

Part Two

THE MODERN AGE

The historical beat continues, but also observations on the mystical side of golf, golf humor, the significance of a big tee ball, why three-putting isn't so bad, and of course, the greatest golf shot ever made

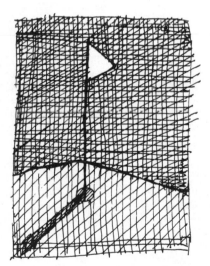

The Importance of Being Arnie

❦

The greatest golf champions are popularizers, and the greater popularizer of all was Arnold Palmer. He was the Brando of golf—muscular, charismatic, with wavy brown hair and boyish good looks. He came from a Pennsylvania steel town, and both steelworkers and country clubbers adored him. He smoked. He drank. He hitched his pants. And the way he played golf had an effect on people like nobody before or since.

George Plimpton describes what it was like to watch Palmer in his prime: "I found myself transfixed by the excitement of it, scarcely believing that it would be possible to walk around a golf course and watch a golfer hit a golf shot and wax enthusiastic about it. Of sporting spectacles a golf stroke is surely the one least adaptable to exhilaration. And yet Palmer made it an art of such excitement."

These days, we know Palmer mainly as a golfing tycoon, one of the world's richest athletes though he hasn't won a major golf tournament for decades. He is the apotheosis of conservatism—owner of a chain of car dealerships, product spokesman, golf figurehead. But the way he played golf was anything but conservative. "He doesn't play a golf course," said the columnist Jim Murray, only half-joking, "he tries to obliterate it."

Palmer's game was an expression of power and drive, an assertion of will. Jack Nicklaus, his greatest rival, said that Palmer tried to "literally force the course into submission and hang the consequences." Jerry Barber, a fellow pro, said, "Palmer grabs a course by the throat and shakes it to death." It seems almost incongruous to use such words as "risk" and "attack" when speaking of so placid a game as golf. But such was Palmer's gift that he gave force and meaning to these words, and in so doing reinvigorated the ancient game. "I could not retreat from a challenge," he wrote in his auto-biography. "If the chance was there, and if—no matter how difficult it appeared—it meant winning, I was going to take it." Charge!

Palmer's back and shoulders and arms were very strong, and he threw himself violently into the act of hitting a golf ball as far as he could possibly make it go. His fellow pros called him the Bull. Yet for all his impressive muscularity—so different from the typical notion of what a golfer should look like—he had a jewelmaker's touch on the green. "If I ever needed an eight-foot putt and everything I owned depended on it, I would want Arnold Palmer to putt it for me," said Bobby Jones, a mighty fair putter himself. Nicklaus said that Palmer in his prime was the best putter he'd ever seen, a talent he attributed to Palmer's enormous strength of will. Bob Rosburg agreed: "The ball's scared of him. He'll get it in the hole if he has to stare it in."

Palmer won the 1958 Masters—his first major—but the year to remember was 1960. Few people in the history of golf have ever had as good a year as Palmer did in 1960. He won the Masters again, and he came within the length of Kel Nagle's whiskers of taking the British Open title. But it was his victory at the U.S. Open at Cherry Hills that year that established him as a new and vividly exciting presence on the national sporting scene. Sam Snead once said about Palmer, "This guy wants to hole out everything from the first tee." On the final day, lining up at the 346-yard 1st hole at Cherry Hills, Palmer almost did, greening his tee shot and going on to score a 30 on the front nine. At the start of the last round, fourteen golfers stood between him and the lead. He was seven strokes down. On the 10th hole he tied Mike Souchak for the lead; two holes later it was Palmer's to keep. "It was the most explosive stretch of subpar golf any golfer has ever produced in the championship," wrote a breathless Herbert Warren Wind afterward.

That 1960 Open was a turning-point event, for the past, present, and future of the game came together on those last, heart-stopping holes. Ben Hogan, an emblem of golf past, courageously challenged for the title but weakened at the end; while Jack Nicklaus, golf future, came close but finished second behind the onrushing Palmer. The present belonged to the brawny, cigarette-smoking matinee idol, who ushered in the modern era with a hitch of his pants and the *thwack!* of his driver. The old order was represented by Hogan and his technically superb, yet conservative brand of golf. Suddenly the old ways seemed stodgy and obsolete, and like all the truly great athletes Arnold came to represent the era in which he performed. Not a few observers have noted that his breakthrough year occurred in 1960, the same year John Kennedy was elected president.

After the Open, Palmer went overseas and did it there, too. At the time the British Open was of little or no consequence to the American golfers who dominated golf. Palmer changed all that, helping to create the idea of four major titles—the PGA, Masters, and the two Opens—that would be the greatest tests of a golfer's skill. Raves Tony Jacklin, "On both sides of the Atlantic he grabbed an ailing game by the scruff of the neck and through the thrilling aggression of his game and a magic appeal, gave golf a new status." Henry Longhurst, another Britisher, said, "He is the man that everyone wants to win." Though he lost that year he came back to Britain in 1961 and 1962 and won back-to-back titles.

Back then Arnold Palmer *was* golf, and for millions of Americans, he still is golf. They may not be able to tell a Faldo from a Kite, but they know about Arnie. Even the most casual fan can probably tell you something about his background—how he came from Latrobe, Pennsylvania, and how his father ran the golf course there and that was how Arnie learned the game. Palmer worked as a caddie and played every chance he got as a boy, and his fabled confidence showed itself when he carried the clubs for the locals who played at the Latrobe course. "I might ask for a four-iron and Arnie'd look up at me like I didn't know what I was doing," recalled one Latrobe businessman from those days. "He'd just shake his head as if he felt sorry for me." The man would then ask, "Well, what club do you think I should use?" and Arnie would tell him. Guess who was usually right.

Arnie became the top man on the Wake Forest University golf team, but after Bud Worsham, a good friend and teammate, died in a car crash, Palmer lost interest in the game and joined the Coast Guard for three years. Gradually his love of golf was rekindled, and after leaving the Coast Guard he won the 1954 U.S. Amateur at Grosse Point Farms, Michigan. There, people began to take notice of the muscular young man who could hit it a ton. "That's Arnold Palmer," said Gene Littler when asked to identify him for the press. "He's going to be a great player someday. When he hits the ball, the earth shakes."

Palmer was the most exciting golfer to watch in the history of the game. In that 1960 Masters he birdied 17 and 18 on the last day and came from behind to win. At the 1963 Los Angeles Open he made up three strokes on the final day and won. At the Texas Open he strung together three birdies on the last four holes and won by a stroke. At the Palm Springs Classic he topped that with five birdies on the five finishing holes. "I have a very uncomfortable feeling when Arnold is behind me breathing down my neck," said Gary Player, expressing the view of many of the pros of the time. "I'd rather be a stroke behind him than a stroke ahead of him."

Meanwhile, Palmer's famous late-round charges and his philosophy of risk galvanized the public. He was, writes Colman McCarthy, "the boldest of the troubleshooters. Four or five times a round he would, like a fallen but vengeful angel, slash his way out of one layer of hell or another. Why settle for a routine birdie, he seemed to be thinking, when you can get a miracle par?" Charles Price said that Palmer approaching the first tee of a golf course was like a heavyweight prize fighter entering the ring before a championship bout—that kind of excitement. He was the general in "Arnie's Army," and his huge, sprawling, rambunctious galleries dwarfed those of his competitors in size and in the expression of their ardor. Everyone wanted to see Arnie play. (One fan went so far as to count how many times Palmer hitched his pants in a tournament—345, per eighteen holes.) At the 1962 Masters, Palmer birdied two of the last three holes to force a playoff. During the playoff, which Palmer won, the ostensibly objective workers at Augusta National strung "GO ARNIE!" signs on scoreboards all around the course. In his heyday his popularity was such that his name was bandied about as a possible candidate for the U.S. Senate or governor of Pennsylvania. Even today, decades after he was a real force on a golf course, Palmer in his sixties still commands enormous attention and large galleries whenever he plays on the Senior Tour or in an exhibition. The people remember, and years later they still want to feel the magic.

"There were two things that made golf appealing to the average man," joked Bob Hope. "Arnold Palmer and the invention of the mulligan." Palmer *was* as popular as the mulligan, through force of personality but also because of sheer happenstance. His arrival on the golf scene coincided with the beginnings of extensive live television coverage of the sport. Alistaire Cooke called him "the first television sports star." (The second may have been Muhammad Ali.) Don Ohlmeyer, the television producer, said that the most important picture in TV golf history was Palmer coming out of the crowd on the final hole at the 1962 British Open at Troon. The picture of Palmer, buoyed along in waves of rock-star-like adulation, conveyed excitement to broadcasters, advertisers, and not least, the millions watching at home. With Palmer as focus and star, television—the greatest popularizer of all and one of the most powerful engines of change in the game today—had come to stay.

With television came money, lots and lots of money, and here again Palmer plays a leading role. Under the guidance of his friend and business partner, Mark McCormack, Palmer became a symbol of wealth and corporate success, flying around the country in his private jet, signing deals, making public appearances, endorsing everything from golf clubs to cars to vacation resorts, lending his name to golf real-estate packages, all the while running his own highly profitable corporation. Some critics say that all these outside business interests distracted him from his golf and caused his game to deteriorate. This may be true, but it's also possible that nobody could sustain his all-out, go-for-broke philosophy of golf—McCormack joked once that Palmer's gravestone should read, "Here lies Arnie Palmer. He always went for the green"—forever. Certainly, his blowup on the last day of the 1966 U.S. Open, throwing away the championship after leading by six strokes with only nine holes to go, ranks as one of the biggest chokes in golf history.

In his recent contribution to golfing's belles letters, Curtis Strange talked about Palmer's impact on the game. Strange, the two-time U.S. Open champion, said that many amateur golfers aren't patient enough on a golf course, and this may be due to the great man's lingering influence. "Part of the problem may have to do with the fact that Arnold Palmer did so much to glamorize aggressive golf with his many head-on collisions with golf courses. . . . The thought of playing safe rarely occurred to Palmer—he was forever trying to push the ball to the green from wherever he happened to find it, whether it was in the middle of the fairway or the middle of the woods."

Nothing against you, Curtis, and you make a good point. Arnie may have turned us all into gamblers, though we lack the tools to succeed at it as he did. But put yourself in our position. You're lying three on a par-5 hole, and you're still about two hundred yards from home. You've just rescued your ball from the clutches of a pine tree and kicked it onto a nice grassy spot on the edge of the fairway. Your wife is cheating on you, your company just hired a twenty-six-year-old Harvard MBA to assess your job performance, and your golf game isn't all that great either. But it's a blue, sunny day, and at the end of that long carpet of green you can see the flag fluttering in a soft breeze.

Now, in your mind's eye, who would you rather be—Curtis
Strange or Arnold Palmer?

Go, Arnie!

P lump Jack

〜〜〜

Before he was Golden Jack he was Plump Jack, a prodigiously talented
young golfer who could hit a ball a country mile but who was dumpy
and overweight and the butt of fat jokes. The young Nicklaus, said
Dan Jenkins, could have won "first prize in a livestock contest." He
was known as Baby Beef, Ohio Fats, and the Fat Man. "When he
first burst into the public eye, he was chubby, wore a crew cut, and
dressed like someone who got his apparel in a close-out sale," said
Bob Hope. At the 1962 U.S. Open, Nicklaus, then twenty-two, wore
shiny olive-green pants that he had bought for twelve dollars. He
wore them all four rounds, including the 36-hole final day. But being
a bad dresser didn't hurt his golf any; he won the Open in his first
year as a pro, in a playoff.

Besides being a big tubby, the young Nicklaus was known as
stuck-up and cocky. But who can blame him? Precious few of his
elders were in his league as a golfer. At the age of ten, in the first
nine holes he ever played, young Jack shot a 51. At thirteen he played
in the national junior championships and won three matches. Two
years later he qualified for the U.S. Amateur. He won the 72-hole
Ohio State Open as a sixteen-year-old, and the next year he made
it into the U.S. Open. At age eighteen, playing in his first PGA Tour
event though still an amateur, he was one stroke off the lead after

two rounds. He fell back over the next two days and finished twelfth overall.

Not since Bobby Jones had a golfer accomplished so much at such a tender age. At nineteen Nicklaus won the U.S. Amateur and at twenty he finished second in the 1960 U.S. Open only two strokes behind the winner. Nicklaus said he wanted to be not only the best golfer in the world, but the best of all time. "I'll be honest about it," he told a reporter. "I want to win more [titles] than Jones. That's what you play for, to separate yourself from the crowd."

Even as a boy Nicklaus was single-minded, intense, devoted to the idea of being the world's best player. He averaged three hundred practice shots a day and played no fewer than eighteen holes. When he got older, he hit five or six hundred balls a day and played fifty-four holes. Nobody worked at it like Jack, nobody wanted it more. His teacher was Jack Grout, and they worked together at Scioto Country Club in Columbus, Ohio. To stop his pupil's head from moving, Grout would assign an assistant to stand in front of Nicklaus holding his hair while he swung. If his head moved, his hair got pulled. Young Jack would cry tears of pain during this exercise, but he kept coming back for more. His capacity for work astounded Grout; it seemed inexhaustible.

Blessed with powerful legs and a strong, albeit pudgy, body, the young Nicklaus was not fooled by his physical gifts as a golfer. Early on he applied himself to learning the whole game—not just slapping balls around like other kids his age, but trying to get inside the workings of a golf course and understand why things were the way they were. "The main reason golf appealed to me so much as a kid was that I could do it by myself, without the dependence on other people that most sports involve," Nicklaus wrote once. "From that simple starting point I became more and more intrigued, as my game improved, by the way in which the elements that make up a golf course determine the type and quality of shots a golfer is called upon to play. Seeking to understand each new hole I encountered, I would try to put myself in the mind of the architect. I'd try to figure out why he had done particular things in particular ways."

Nicklaus kept an index card with information on every course he played. Before a tournament he'd consult his files and decide how to approach the course. He was a thinking golfer, as disciplined and focused as Hogan, and yet he could bang with the best of them. He was, say the experts, the longest *straight* driver ever, a man who could "hit a one-iron so high it would stop on concrete," according to Gary Player. At the 1965 Masters, Nicklaus was twenty-five years old and no one on heaven or earth could touch him as a golfer. He shot a third-round 64, tying a quarter-century-old course record. He broke Ben Hogan's tournament record by three strokes with a 271. And he annihilated the rest of the field—the best golfers in the world— by nine strokes. Afterward Bobby Jones—*that* Bobby Jones—said, "The other players here play golf very well. Mr. Nicklaus plays a game with which I am not familiar."

Yet for all his undisputed mastery of the game, the chunky kid with the blond crew cut and bad fashion sense was hardly beloved by the American sporting public. As a matter of fact a good many of them would just as soon have boiled him in oil. The reason? He was beating the pants off their number one hero, a fellow named Palmer.

Rivalry
(Nicklaus-Palmer)

∽◈◌

Golf is a test of skill against the course, not the person or persons you're playing with. This is what separates it from other sports. The challenge is not in beating another individual (we're talking medal play here), but in beating Old Man Par. What is at issue in a game of golf is not your opponent's limitations, but your own. You must learn to disregard the play of others, because if you personalize the game, you're a goner. You may indeed whip the fellow you're aiming at, but in the meantime several others will have passed you and your game will be in a shambles.

All this is certainly true, but it's not the whole story. Tournament golf in the past century is filled with hard-nosed, take-your-best-shot-fella rivalries, with the golf course providing mere backdrop to the vivid interaction of one man (or woman) competing against another. Rivalries help define the era in which they take place: Hagen-Jones, Hagen-Sarazen, Hogan-Snead, Palmer-Nicklaus, Nicklaus-Watson. Until recent years Nicklaus's rivalries have served as a short course in the modern history of the game—first with Arnold Palmer, then Lee Trevino, then in those epic clashes at Turnberry and elsewhere with Tom Watson. The best rivalries in the early nineties are Beth Daniel and Patty Sheehan for the women, and Nick Faldo and Greg Norman for the men, and they're pretty good, too.

But the Daniel-Sheehan and Faldo-Norman combos are going to have go some to match what Arnie and Jack did in the early sixties. That one was the best, the greatest rivalry of all time, and it's not just nostalgia talking either. Time after time they delivered some of the best golf anybody has ever played, and they did it with everything on the line in the biggest tournaments in the world knowing full well that if they let down for just a moment the other guy—*that* guy —would burst in through the front door and claim the title as his own.

Palmer's famous charge won him the 1960 U.S. Open at Cherry Hills. In back of him by two strokes was Nicklaus. Nicklaus led the tournament late on the final day, but he took bogeys on 13 and 14 and succumbed, like everybody else, to Palmer's finishing rush. Two years later it was a different story at the Open. Nicklaus, in those dreadfully ugly green pants, and Palmer finished dead-even after seventy-two holes, but in the playoff Jack the Fashion Victim bested Arnie the Pants Hitcher by three strokes, 71 to 74.

From a public relations standpoint, this was probably the worst thing the young Nicklaus could do for himself. Any other twenty-two-year-old who had been properly brought up by his parents would've had the decency to take a fall for Palmer, who, after all, was the most popular golfer in America and after Jack Kennedy and Marilyn Monroe and a couple of others, may have been the most popular person. But Jack did not lose that playoff to Arnie, and it took years before the public forgave him for it.

In describing golf in the sixties, Lance Compa, writing in a golf magazine, touches on the public's view of Nicklaus: "We were into the late sixties and Palmer was in eclipse. A pudgy, plodding, efficient Ohioan named Nicklaus was golf's king now. Some king. This was the Age of Aquarius—Don't Trust Anyone Over Thirty, Broadway Joe, the Amazin' Mets, Yaz, the Grateful Dead, and the Airplane. But the Golden Bear? Forget it." People resented Nicklaus because success had come at such a young age, and apparently so easily. Not only did he not look the part of a hero, he was not acting it either. He was making a difficult game look ridiculously easy, and he was doing it at the expense of a man who had put the zing back into the heartstrings of the game, a man adored by all.

"There was a certain strain," Nicklaus admits now, looking back on those years. "I was winning the big ones, but people found a reason to belittle me personally. I was not built the way Arnie was, and I could never match his appeal." If Fat Jack grimaced or looked sullen, he was criticized for being moody and unapproachable. If he loosened up and smiled, he was mocked for trying to copy Arnold. Fat Jack couldn't win, except on a golf course, and this was what burned Palmer's fans the most.

The rivalry between the two men themselves was mainly good-natured. They teamed together to win the World Cup four times and were friendly enough so that after Palmer came in with a 75 at a tournament, Nicklaus might joke, "Hey, Arnie, where'd you get all those birdies?" Arnold made occasional jabs at Jack's penchant for slow play, a complaint voiced not by Palmer alone. Nicklaus, he said, "stands over a putt for one or two eternities." Another time he said that Jack's "approach to every shot reminds me of an airline captain doing an exhaustive cockpit check." Palmer once lodged an official complaint about his rival's slow play at a U.S. Open.

Both Palmer and Nicklaus were fiercely competitive men who hated to lose, and sometimes this fierceness displayed itself. One year Palmer won the Bob Hope Desert Classic after Nicklaus missed a tie for first when his eagle putt on the 72nd hole lipped the cup and rolled out.

At the awards ceremonies afterward, Palmer, referring to that barely missed putt, said, "What were you trying to do out there, Jack?"

Arnold was joking. Jack was not. "I was trying to beat you," he said, unsmiling.

On a practice round before the 1967 Open, Nicklaus shot a 62. Asked by a reporter if Nicklaus's hot score bothered him, Palmer said, "I can't imagine anybody being shook up by that round unless it was Jack. Because he didn't get it when it counted."

When informed of these remarks, Nicklaus replied, "Well, I think I'd rather have my sixty-two than what Arnold shot in practice today."

Nicklaus settled the argument by winning the tournament, besting his debating opponent by four strokes.

Ultimately, winning is what shuts everybody up, and if you stick around long enough and do it with as much consistency over the years as Nicklaus has, eventually the public is going to come around and see things your way. (Losing twenty-five pounds and getting a new haircut helps, too.) Even so, while Nicklaus is universally admired for all his major titles and golfing prowess, in certain quarters Arnold Palmer will, always and forevermore, be The Man. Peter Andrews tells the story about an old man who was at Augusta National that day in 1986 when Nicklaus, age forty-six and considered washed-up by many experts, stormed back from deep in the pack to shoot a 65 and win his sixth, and most improbable, Masters. The old man saw the whole thing, but he wasn't impressed. "I don't care what you say," he said to his friend as they were leaving Augusta at the end of the day. "He's not Arnold Palmer and I guarantee he never will be."

The Big Drive

From time to time Big Arnie and Big Jack put down the Big Drive, although, of course, their fortunes and their reputations rest on it. Palmer likes to emphasize the direction of the ball—i.e., straight— over pure distance, adding that the power hitter must learn to think his way around the course else all that long driving will be for naught. Nicklaus can be a similar sort of nag. When he thinks back on the big tournaments he's played in and all the great shots he's made to win them, what sticks in his mind, he says, are not the times he's knocked the hell out of the ball—but instead, "the approaches, recoveries, and putts" that have figured significantly in his victories. Quoth Jack: "I could describe such shots, good and bad, all day, but drives fade quickly from my mind." And this, from a fellow who *averaged* 260-yarders off the tee and changed balls five or six times a round because his hard swinging knocked them out of shape.

That both Jack and Arnie would, at least in their spoken pronouncements, put the knock on the Big Drive is to be expected. They don't want to be known simply as bashers; they want to be seen as complete golfers, guys who could move the ball around and put it where they wanted it to go rather than just hit it a long way. Nevertheless, coming from two of the heaviest hitters in golf history, you have to take such talk with a grain of salt. There's a story making the rounds about how Nicklaus and Greg Norman were playing with Jumbo Osaki in Japan, and Jumbo was cracking his drives well down the fairway past the other two. "Hey, wait a minute," said Greg and Jack, "what's going on here?" What is going on here, said Jumbo, is this new lickin' stick I'm using. So Greg and Jack got their hands on "J's Professional Weapon," and their tee balls started flying thirty and forty yards farther down the track, too. Or so goes the legend anyhow.

The point of this story is not that Jumbo's "Professional Weapon" is the greatest golf club since little Sammy Snead tore a branch off a swamp-maple tree in the backwoods of Virginia—it may, in fact, be no different from any of the other high-tech marvels being sold on the market today. No, the point is that both Nicklaus and Norman *thought* it might be, and that has little to do with the club itself and quite a bit to do with the inextinguishable yearning, on the part of all of us, to hit the ball farther.

The Big Drive—or more exactly, the Lure of the Big Drive—is here to stay. Big Arnie, Big Jack, and Big Greg could gather Big Nick, Big Payne, Big Seve, Big Curtis, and all the other big cheeses together for a Vatican II on golf. They could meet, and from on high they could issue a joint proclamation decrying the emphasis on the Big Drive and asking golfers the world over to concentrate more on their pitching and their chipping and their putting. But it wouldn't matter. People would still want to blast that ball three hundred yards and worry about the other stuff later.

The Big Drive, in golf, is like the home run in baseball or the ninety-nine-yard touchdown bomb in football. It has to do with expanding limits, and defying them. When Greg Norman stands up and hits one out of sight, it is a pioneering act; that ball is going where no ball has gone before, and riding on that tiny little dimpled spaceship are the hopes and dreams of anybody who has ever pulled a 1-wood out of a bag. We've heard all the warnings many times: "Drive for show, putt for dough"; "There's nothing unusual about long hitters. The woods are full of them"; etc. But still, it's the Big Drive that beckons and calls out to us. Why? Just ask Edmund Hillary. Because it's there.

We admire putters and chippers; but we want to *be* long hitters. A drive is an assertion; putting is a hope. Putting is black magic that no one can understand. A drive is applied knowledge. It's not simply an expression of power, as some might think. It's an expression of power and stroke and rhythm, harnessed on behalf of a clear and defined goal. A putt counts for a stroke but may only travel a few inches. A drive counts for one stroke, too, but it can travel 250, 275, 300 yards or more. Now that's a stroke! You get your money's worth when you take a stroke like that, unlike a putt, which, of course, holds the secret to good scoring on a golf course but is more frustrating and far less rewarding even when successful.

A drive, however, can also be an extremely embarrassing thing when it fails to come off as planned, which is quite often the case. And the most humiliating moment in all of golf may be when a man or woman steps up to the tee and instead of hitting the Big Drive, hits nothing at all. You feel so completely alone, and so utterly foolish. It happened to one husky fellow who, while whiffing his tee shot, brought up a chunk of earth that covered his ball. Knowing that he had missed the ball, but not finding it anywhere, the man lapsed into a sudden panic: "Where is it? Where is it?" he cried, until it was pointed out to him that his ball lay hidden underneath his divot. The man smiled weakly and quickly hit again, this time with somewhat more success.

Curses!

One of the more notable sidelights to a game of golf is the opportunity to hear a man curse—really air out those lungs and let loose with some truly foul language. It's one of the game's least-appreciated skills. The pros talk about a proper follow-through, but a volley of unprintable cuss words can be a far more satisfactory end to a golf shot.

Golfers number among the leading citizens in every community across the land—teachers, doctors, business professionals, officers of government, ministers. But put a golf club in their hands and they become as foulmouthed as any longshoreman who can make a mermaid dance by wiggling the muscles of his forearm. A longshoreman? A golfer in the heat of a bad game can outswear a longshoreman any day.

Want to know how much a golfer swears? Go out to your garage and get a hammer. Bring the hammer back into your kitchen. Place one hand down on the kitchen table and with your other hand, slam the hammer directly onto your fingers resting on the table. *That* is close to what golfers sound like when they're out on the links.

Cursing can break down barriers on a golf course. You may feel uncomfortable with the person you're playing with, someone you don't know very well. But if he should happen to chili-dip a ball across the green into a trap and then unloose with some high-voltage profanity—assuming his foul mood doesn't carry over and poison your game—you will probably find yourselves more relaxed around each other, more in synch.

One year at the Masters, Tony Lema was having a heckuva time of it. He couldn't do anything right and expressed himself accordingly. After a minute or so of haranguing the heavens he noticed that his playing partner, a Taiwanese golfer by the name of Chen Ching-po, was staring at him. "Uh, excuse me," said Lema. "I have to apologize. I really shouldn't use that kind of language in front of a visitor to our country."

"It's all right," said Chen, who was smiling. "If I knew those words, I'd use them myself."

Terrible Tommy Bolt

Without doubt, the greatest club thrower in the modern history of the game was Tommy Bolt, whose club-tossing and club-breaking spectacles in the late 1950s and 1960s are the stuff of golf legend. Terrible Tommy. Tommy "Thunder" Bolt. Tantrum Tom. He had the temper of Zeus and the patience of a two-year-old. "I guess I do have a pretty low boiling point," he said once, "but I haven't broken as many as people think. Only a dozen or so." Only a dozen? Tom, you sell yourself short.

Henry Longhurst wrote, "The most exquisitely satisfying act in the world of golf is that of throwing a club." If so, Tommy was an exquisitely satisfied man. It was said that Bolt threw clubs into the turf with such force that it took two people to pull them out. He snapped clubs over his knee. After three-putting a green he would stop and smash his putter against a tree before walking on to the next hole.

If a club was not performing well for him, Bolt got rid of it. He was on the 16th fairway at Pebble Beach about 130 yards from the hole when he asked his caddie for a 9-iron. The caddie offered him a 3-wood or a 4-iron. Bolt asked again for the 9, and the caddie once more offered the wood or the 4-iron.

"Listen, fella," said Bolt, irritated. "I asked for the nine-iron. Now give it to me."

"But Mr. Bolt," replied the caddie, "these two are all that's left in your bag."

At another tournament Bolt and his caddie disagreed about which club to use. Bolt said the 5-iron, the caddie said the 6. "You're crazy," said Bolt, who used the 5-iron and hit the ball into a lake. Furious, he snapped the club over his knee and stormed off. His caddie, still holding the correct 6-iron, then snapped the club over *his* knee and stormed off in the opposite direction.

A native Oklahoman, Bolt was not a guy to mess with on a golf course. On the 18th hole at Pebble during the Crosby Pro-Am, Bolt was about to putt when he heard the whirring sound of a motor-drive camera. He stalked over and confronted the female perpetrator: "Lady, why are you doing this to me? I wouldn't barge into your kitchen and crack my knuckles while you're making biscuits, would I?" He once accosted a writer for getting his age wrong in an article; the newspaper printed it as forty-nine instead of the correct thirty-nine. The writer explained that it was a typographical error, but Tommy wasn't having any of it. "Typographical error, my ass!" he fumed. "That was a perfect '4' and a perfect '9'!"

Golf was serious business to Tommy. That may be why he got so mad when he played poorly. After missing three putts in a row at a major tournament, he raised up and shook his fist at the heavens. "Come down here and fight like a man!" he yelled. Playing for the U.S. in the 1957 Ryder Cup, he and his opponent, a Scot, hated each other so much it was suggested that they settle their differences not by golf, but by throwing clubs at fifty paces. Based on Bolt's experience, it might not have been a fair fight.

Arnold Palmer, who was cured of a club-throwing habit as a youngster after his father threatened to take his clubs away if he ever did it again, was once quoted as saying that *he* never made a bad shot in his life; it was always his clubs that did it. Palmer may have been kidding, but Bolt, who was of a similar bent, wasn't. Like a teacher admonishing a pupil for acting up in class, he frequently had to punish his clubs for bad behavior. He may have broken more clubs than any other pro in recent history, and the ones he didn't break, he threw for record distance. At an exhibition in Latin America, Bolt asked his son to demonstrate what he had learned from him. His son stepped up and tossed a club twenty yards. A spiritual descendant of such club-throwing craftsmen as Ky Laffoon, Ivan Gantz, and Lefty Stackhouse, Bolt advanced the art to new levels, demonstrating that it was far more efficient to toss a club in front of you rather than flipping it behind you. That way, you wouldn't have to walk back to get it; you could pick it up on your way to the green.

His most famous club-throwing incident came in 1960 at the U.S. Open at Cherry Hills in Denver, a moment captured for all time in a photograph by John Zimmerman. In the photo Bolt, who won the Open two years before, is seen in full fury, raising his driver over his head and lunging at the lake at 18 as if he had just seen a snake in the water and was trying to kill it. "Considering the size, beauty, and beckoning nature of the water hazard," wrote Herbert Warren Wind, who was on hand to witness it, "there was something classic about Bolt's performance, like Hillary scaling Everest or Stanley finding Livingstone." Bolt got into this overheated state by hitting a ball into a lake on the 12th hole and arguing with an official about his drop. By three-putting the next hole and bogeying the one after that. And on 18, by hitting not one but two drives into the lake. Since that was where his ball apparently wanted to go, Bolt figured that his driver belonged there, too, and in an expressive bit of pique that still warms the hearts of all of us who have done or wanted to do the same thing, he threw the damn thing into the water.

In Praise of Stuffed Shirts

❧

When I reach sixty, I'm gonna buy a blue blazer
and a can of dandruff and run the USGA.

—*Lee Trevino*

Every year, much like the swallows of San Juan Capistrano, the best golfers in the world migrate to the site of the U.S. Open to (1) test their skills against their contemporaries and (2) to bitch up a storm, though not necessarily in that order. The bitching is about the golf course they're being forced to play, a course prepared according to the age-old USGA specifications of narrow fairways, fast, hard greens, and high rough that can barely be negotiated with a machete, let alone a wedge. The USGA has been setting up its courses this way since before Lee Trevino was in short pants, and the players, bless their hearts, have been complaining about it for just as long.

"Nobody ever wins the Open," said Bobby Jones. "Somebody else loses it." At the 1930 Open at Interlachen, which Jones did not lose, nearly a third of the players shot 80 or better on the final round. Jones hit a ball into the rough bordering the 17th green; the rough was so deep that although thousands of people were looking on, no one could find the ball.

Clayton Heafner, who finished second in a pair of Opens after World War II, hated the Open courses with a passion. He dreamed of leading the Open and needing only a one-foot putt on the final green to win. He'd then pick up his ball and toss it into the gallery. "Fuck it," he'd say as he walked past the flabbergasted USGA officials, never to return.

For the 1951 Open at Oakland Hills Country Club in Birmingham, Michigan, Robert Trent Jones remodeled an old Donald Ross layout and turned it into perhaps the toughest Open course ever. This was the course that Ben Hogan, in his famous remark, labeled "a monster," adding, "If I had to play this course for a living every week, I'd get into another business." Hogan shot a final-round 67, one of only two men (our man Heafner was the other) to break par on a round for the entire four days. Cary Middlecoff, one of those who did not fare so well at the tournament, said that "we had to walk single file down the fairway to stay out of the rough."

In defense of the setup at Oakland Hills, the chairman of the greens committee said, "The Open is the greatest title there is. The course should be so hard, nobody can win it." This is an essential element of the yearly Open ritual as well. The pros attack the course, while the officials, citing tradition and the upholding of standards, defend it.

As the dominant player of the 1950s, Hogan became the inspiration for the type of courses favored by the USGA. The Iceman played a precision game: straight tee balls, keep it out of the fringe, no mistakes. The USGA in turn sought to reward discipline on the golf course, and to punish the hell out of anyone who did not exercise it. In 1970, at another Robert Trent Jones design in Hazeltine, Minnesota, Dave Hill excoriated the Open course as "a cowpatch" after finishing his second round. Asked what it was lacking, Hill said, "All it needs is eighty acres of corn and a few cows. They ruined a good farm when they built this course." What, then, should they do about it, Dave? "Plow it over and start over," he told reporters. For the next two days some of the locals followed Hill around the course making mooing sounds. Despite all, he finished second for the tournament, his highest finish ever at a U.S. Open.

In 1973, Johnny Miller's final round 63 at Oakmont sent USGA pacemakers whizzing into overdrive. The next year the blue coats sought revenge. Determined not to see a recurrence of Miller's feat, they went to work on Winged Foot, and when they were done, almost nobody shot 75 or under on the opening round. Asked if the USGA was trying to embarrass the best golfers in the world, one official replied, "We're not trying to embarrass the best players. We're trying to identify them."

The USGA is nothing if not consistent. Faced with another set of criticisms at another Open a few years ago, an executive director explained why he enjoyed the sight of golfers wading through jungle-type rough: "I like to see them get their socks wet. I want them to be reminded every step of the way that this is the U.S. Open."

Indeed. As much as we like to mock them, the stuffed shirts of the USGA are doing exactly what they should be doing—and exactly what we want them to. "Who needs compassion at a U.S. Open?" writes the journalist E. M. Swift. "When a player flies into the weeds, the world wants to see him start hacking. We want to see beads of sweat around his corporate visor and hear his muffled curses about cows and cornfields."

In other words, boys, suffer.

But the USGA should not keep doing what it's doing just to give vicarious thrills to all the people who've suffered on a golf course and who now want to see the pampered, overpaid, so-called greatest in the world take their lumps, too. The USGA should keep doing what it's doing for one reason above all: *the Open means something.* In a circuit besotted with AT&Ts, Nabiscos and GTEs, one indistinguishable from the next, the Open is special. And with the integrity of its 18-hole playoff format intact, it is unique among all the majors. The pros know it, and that's why for all their complaining, they keep coming back.

The year was 1964, and the Open was being held in stifling heat and humidity at the Congressional Country Club in Washington, D.C. At that time the final thirty-six holes were all played on Saturday, and in the morning round Ken Venturi, a thirty-three-year-old San Franciscan, shot a 66 to pull within two strokes of the lead. But between rounds a doctor advised him to stop playing. Under the severe conditions, said the doctor, Venturi was risking his life if he continued.

Once a talented amateur who had very nearly won the 1956

Masters, Venturi was not about to quit despite experiencing dehydration and intense fatigue. He had come too long and too far for that. He had survived a bad car accident in 1961. He had overcome a debilitating back injury and a drinking problem and the near total collapse of his game to climb back into contention for the lead of the Open. He stayed in the tournament, and with the doctor accompanying him for all eighteen holes, he shot a heat-defying 70 and won by four strokes. The exhaustion and strain were evident in his face and body as he trudged slowly up to the 18th green. After sinking his final putt Venturi dropped his putter and said, "My God, I've won the Open." Many of his fellow pros broke down in tears at this moment. Venturi had won the greatest honor in golf, fulfilling a dream shared by them all.

The Crosby

The Crosby is an emblem of what's fun about golf—and what may be missing from today's PGA Tour. One year on a Saturday night snow fell on the California coast. "I knew I got loaded last night," said Jimmy Demaret, waking up the next morning and seeing the ground covered with white, "but how did I wind up at Squaw Valley?"

It wasn't Squaw Valley, it was the Monterey Peninsula and it was a time—and a scene—that has gone away for good. They hold another tournament there now and it appears to be a reasonable facsimile of the Crosby. It's held, like the Crosby, on the gorgeous, wind-whipped, ocean-drenched, heaven-blessed Monterey Peninsula. It attracts movie stars, big-time athletes, and knights of commerce just as the Crosby did.

But it's not the same. No sirree, Bing. The Crosby Clambake was something else.

One of the things people talked about when they talked about the Crosby was the weather. Year after year one of the tour's most beautiful settings provided the most hellacious atmospherics: wind, rain, fog, sleet, and as Demaret witnessed, even snow. One day at Cypress Point the wind was blowing so hard it knocked down the starter's stand. "Jeez," said an awestruck Jack Burke. "You'd think Bing would call this thing off today." Lawson Little, playing with Burke, scoffed. Little had won the U.S. Open and the Crosby and he considered himself no pansy. "You young guys," he said to Burke. "A little bad weather hits, and you want to run inside." By the 3rd hole, Little's umbrella had blown inside out. At 16, after hitting into gale-force winds and hooking four straight drives into the ocean, he turned to Burke and grumbled, "You'd think Bing would want to call this thing off, wouldn't you?"

Golfers talk about two of the three Crosby courses—Pebble Beach and Cypress Point—in the same hushed, worshipful tones that churchgoers reserve for the deity. (Because it would not alter its membership policies to allow minorities and women, Cypress Point was removed as a tournament site and replaced by Poppy Hills following the 1990 season.) One prominent USGA official called Cypress "the Sistine Chapel of golf." Ken Venturi said, "It's the closest place to me that you can get to God." Porky Oliver was surely not so reverential the time he took a sixteen on the 16th at Cypress, the famous one where you have to shoot across the water and hope it clears the cliffs. Fighting a stiff wind, Porky, who once won the Crosby, dropped a handful of shots into the Pacific before getting stuck in the ball-eating ice plant along the cliffs. "In my book," said his partner who witnessed the debacle, "Porky didn't make a bad shot among those sixteen." Porky may not have made a bad shot, but he did make a lot of them.

Another time on the fabled 16th at Cypress, Henry Ransom struck three shots into the cliffs, the last of which ricocheted off a rock and hit him in the stomach. "That's it," he said, throwing his club down and storming off the course and out of the tournament. "When they start hitting back at you, it's time to quit."

Pebble Beach is another course that inspires golfing awe. Payne Stewart, the beknickered pro, called it "the prettiest place to play golf in the world." A San Francisco amateur named Matt Palacios would go Stewart one better and admit to thoughts of a higher presence at Pebble. Palacios once hit a drive that was heading straight for the ocean. "Only God can save that one," he said. No sooner did the words leave his lips than the waves parted and the ball hit a rock, bouncing out of harm's way onto the fairway. "Thank you, God," said Palacios.

Naturally, along with the weather and the scenery, the Crosby was known for its celebrities. In its heyday in the fifties and early sixties it was the hippest thing going—a golfing party. "This is the place for the elite, where ocean and golf ball meet," said Bob Hope, who was a regular. Wealthy socialites, golfers, business executives on a starry-eyed holiday, artists, athletes, local Carmel people—all rubbed shoulders and clinked glasses with the biggest names in Hollywood. There were parties all the time. Soirees at Francis Brown's or the Ketchams', Jimmy Hatlo's Sunday brunch in a tent by the 7th green, and the raucous Clambake on Saturday night. Back when he was in the army and stationed at nearby Fort Ord, a young nobody by the name of Clint Eastwood snuck into the Clambake dinner, posing as a sportswriter's assistant. He ate steak and gobbled dessert. Now, of course, Eastwood is one of the star attractions at the tournament.

The stars Eastwood might have seen that night in 1952 were from an older Hollywood generation, stars whose time in the spotlight has, by and large, passed. Dean Martin, Phil Harris, Mickey Rooney, Hoagy Carmichael on late-night piano, Randolph Scott, Tennessee Ernie Ford, Hope, and Crosby. Ah, but the times they had! The drinks, the jokes, the great golf (oh, well, two out of three). We should all be so lucky.

The stars, probably more so than the golf, were the chief item of interest for the galleries at the Crosby. Where else could you get within arm's reach of so many legends of the silver screen? But the atmosphere was relaxed, convivial, decidedly not Hollywood, and the legends being gawked at enjoyed themselves as much as the gawkers.

Early one morning at Pebble the starter was calling for Johnny Weissmuller, the first and greatest Tarzan the Ape Man. "Calling Johnny Weissmuller, calling Johnny Weissmuller," the starter intoned four or five times, until Don Cherry, who was trying to sleep in after a late night of carousing, flung open his window at the Del Monte Lodge and shouted, "Damn it, if you want Weissmuller, just look up in the tree!" Bing got off a pretty good Tarzan line, too, after hitting a ball that got stuck out of reach between the branches of a cypress tree. "Where the heck is Johnny Weissmuller when you need him?" he joked. Then there was the time Weissmuller himself climbed a tree to retrieve one of his balls, swung from a branch, and let out his famous ape call.

Phil Harris was a Crosby fixture. Though he played—he and Dutch Harrison once won the pro-am—he was better known as a lovable lush and in later years, became "social director" of the event. At the Crosby, "social directing" meant making sure everyone's glasses were filled.

Harris may have been in the car that night when a bunch of the regulars, including Bing, had to drive home after a party at Francis Brown's that didn't break up until dawn's early light. The revelers piled into the backseat while a snookered Bing drove and his son Lindsay, sober but only thirteen years old, sat uncertainly beside him. They made it all right, but barely. Asked later why he had let his father drive in such a condition, Lindsay responded, "He was the best we had."

It was Bing—the man with the golden vocal cords, Father O'Malley, Mr. White Christmas—who held it all together, and although members of his family remain associated with the tournament, the fact that he's gone is undoubtedly why it's not the same. The ocean, the rain, the celebs, the parties (though now mainly corporate-sponsored), the gorgeous courses—but no Bing. Sorry, it just isn't the same deal.

Harry Lillis Crosby, who died of a heart seizure just after completing a round of golf, often played in a tweed hat while smoking a pipe. He caddied as a boy and played throughout his life. While in vaudeville in New York City during the twenties, he and Bob Hope would go out between shows and hit balls at a Fifty-ninth Street driving range. Crosby left New York for Hollywood and there took up the game seriously, becoming a member of Lakeside Country Club, the in club for the movie set. Before going to Paramount to work each day, Crosby would get up early and play a fast eighteen. "He had the slowest backswing I've ever seen," Hope once wrote of his pal. "While he was taking the club back, you could fit him for a tailored suit." Unlike Hope, Crosby was a first-rate golfer. He played to a two handicap and reportedly hated to lose.

With the tournament bearing his name, Crosby invented the celebrity pro-am. The tournament started at Rancho Santa Fe near San Diego in 1937 (Sam Snead was the first winner), and after the war it moved to the Monterey Peninsula, where it flourished. In the beginning, the idea was this: Bing would invite some of his friends over for a little golf with the touring pros, guys who really knew what they were doing out there. Then afterward in the evening they'd get together and have a few laughs. The Crosby got bigger over the years, but it always stayed true to its original idea. Golf, friends, lots of laughs. The Crosby was something else. So was its founder.

The Man Who Never Makes the Cut

I would rather open on Broadway in Hamlet,
*with no rehearsals, than tee off at Pebble Beach
in the tournament.*

—*Jack Lemmon*

In golf, Jack Lemmon shall forever be known as the man who never makes the cut. Every year he comes to the Monterey Peninsula to play in the Pebble Beach Pro-Am; every year he misses the cut. People throng to see him not make the cut. They would be disappointed if he ever did.

"Lemmon the golfer is so much like Lemmon the screen persona," Jack Sheehan writes. "An average man struggling to make sense of a maddening, impersonal world." One television analyst found eleven major flaws in Lemmon's stroke; he would've found more except he stopped counting. One year at Pebble Beach, Lemmon hit a wind-blown drive that sailed fifty yards over the green. "That's the best shot you've hit all day," said his partner, the actor James Garner. "Unfortunately, it's in the ocean."

Lemmon, the star of *The Apartment, Save the Tiger, Some Like It Hot, Missing*, and so many other wonderful movies, was a fisherman, not a golfer, when he was a kid. He took the game up in his thirties, in the beginning using a set of clubs handed down to him by his father. The hickory-shaft driver was a basket case; the wrapper was peeling off and it lacked pins to hold it together. One day when he went to hit with it the head spun completely around like a top, and his ball spurted about twenty yards into the rough—an act of unintentional slapstick that convulsed Jack Benny, who was looking on. Jack Lemmon, the golfer, has been making people laugh—and wince—ever since.

Bing Crosby, watching Lemmon swing a club, said he "looks like he's basting a chicken." "His backswing," said one wit, "is shorter than his cigar." Lemmon, added Phil Harris, "has been in more bunkers than Eva Braun." In fairness, though, few of us have had our golfing mistakes witnessed by so many people and under such trying conditions. At Pebble, besides the spectators, there are all those television cameras. One year Lemmon four-putted a green while watching helplessly as one of the putts came rolling back downhill through his legs. Another time he hit two tee shots out-of-bounds and reached the green in nine. Surveying his thirty-foot putt, Lemmon asked his caddie which way he thought it would break. "Who cares?" the caddie replied.

Celebrity Golf

The best-known golf swing in Hollywood today belongs to Johnny Carson, who cues the band at the end of each "Tonight Show" monologue with a wristy air shot that seems to lack adequate follow-through. Johnny probably needs to consult a pro on his grip, too. It is too loose and relaxed, even for late night. His left hand needs to be in a stronger clockwise position, and he should eliminate the spaces between his thumb, the forefinger of his hand and the club, which, of course, in this case, does not exist at all. Johnny's poor execution may be due to the fact that he is a tennis player, not a golfer, and not up on the latest developments in modern swing theory.

If he *were* interested in improving his game—even an imaginary one—but hesitant about consulting a pro, Johnny could very easily turn to fellow members of the entertainment community, a tiny minority of whom are passable as golfers. Unfortunately, many are not. The way most Hollywood personalities play golf is remindful of tour pro Lloyd Mangrum's assessment of comedian George Burns forty years ago: "You look perfect," Mangrum told Burns. "That beautiful shirt, alpaca sweater, those expensive slacks. It's a damned shame you have to spoil it by playing golf."

Despite their inadequacies, some of Hollywood's biggest stars have taken to golf over the years like bees to honey. First there was Bing and his famous tournament, and if Bing had one, you knew Bob had to get one, too, and if Bing and Bob both had one, Frank sure as heck could have one, for it's well known that Frank could have anything he wanted, at least in the old days. And if Frank had one, you knew it was only a matter of time before Sammy and Dean got theirs, and if you're talking singers, who can dig down and belt one out like Andy "Moon River" Williams? Andy joined Bing, Bob, Frank, Sammy, Dean, and guitar-plucking Glen, who may have been the best golfer in the bunch, but that hardly mattered because when Dinah got hers, she was a tennis player. That fun-loving Gleason had one (quoth Bob: "He's the only guy I know with a spigot on his five-iron. His caddie doubles as a bartender"), and you had to make room for Danny Thomas, too. There were Jerry and his kids, Garagiola and the baseball crowd, the brothers Gatlin, and even Jamie "Corporal Klinger" Farr, who once putted at Dinah's tournament using his nose.

Dinah Shore, whose event is one of the LPGA's majors and whose profound contribution to golf is well known, summed up her fascination with the game this way: "It's the most humbling sport ever. It's like a lousy lover. It's like some guy who's never there when you need him. Every once in a while he comes and makes you feel like heaven on earth. And then the moment you say, 'I really need this,' he's gone." Jack Benny, who never hosted a golf tournament but had a successful show business career in spite of it, expressed his feelings about the game in a similar but different vein: "Give me good golf clubs, fresh air, and a beautiful partner, and you can keep my clubs and the fresh air."

Jocks Who Play

Golf has always been the off-season sport of preference for jocks and the men and women who pay them. The jocks like it for the same reasons everyone else does; it's fun and relaxing, a nice way to spend a Saturday afternoon. The people who pay the jocks like golf too, because, unlike other potential leisure-time activities—skiing, off-road racing, bungie jumping—their stadium-packing, crowd-pleasing, revenue-enhancing superstars probably won't get hurt playing it. It's standard that professional athletes have clauses in their contracts forbidding them from participating in certain high-risk recreational pursuits in the off-season. Golf is not one of them, its primary health risk being a head-on collision with a golf ball, which, to my knowledge, has yet to occur to any of our golf-playing athletic superstars.

These days, it seems, anybody with a .263 batting average who can make the pivot at second base has taken up golf and is hosting his own pro-am. Baseball players, hockey players, football players, basketball players—they're all out there, and they've got an advantage over the rest of us because they have large chunks of time in their off months to devote to the game. John Elway, the Broncos' Super

Bowl–haunted quarterback, plays and plays well, according to authoritative sources. Mark Rypien, signal-caller for the Redskins, is also reportedly very good, as is Phil Simms of the Giants. Simms and a teammate on the Giants, head-crunching linebacker Lawrence Taylor, will sneak in nine holes between practices at training camp. The work is apparently paying off for L.T.; he can drive the ball over 400 yards and once nearly greened a 430-yard tee shot in a Florida tourney. Dan Marino of the Dolphins has expressed his golf philosophy thusly: "Swing hard in case you hit it," and Jim McMahon, the former bad-boy quarterback for the Bears, likes to play in his bare feet. These two seem to take their golf less seriously than Taylor, but then they probably never hit a 400-yard tee shot either.

(Stories about the heavy-thumping Lawrence Taylor recall the golfing exploits of another big-time jock, Alex Karras, the former Detroit Lions tackle and "Monday Night Football" announcer. Karras, who played on the defensive line and was a pretty meaty guy himself, was teeing off at a course in Royal Oak, Michigan. But the ball went off the end of his club and went flying through a huge plate glass window at the clubhouse restaurant. The entire window came down with a crash, although fortunately the restaurant was empty at the time and no one was hurt. At the sound of the crash a man in the dining-room kitchen came running in, and he couldn't believe what he saw: broken glass everywhere. The man also noticed a head poking through what had formerly been the front window of the restaurant. It belonged to Alex Karras. "Hey," said Karras, "is this room out-of-bounds?")

"With golf you get a chance to reveal something about your character because of the challenge of great courses," says Julius Erving, the wondrous basketball star who took up golf, largely for business reasons, after he retired. "It's also an education about what's going on in another man's mind. How does he approach a position you were in?" If golf gives you a look into another man's mind, what does that say about someone such as Doug Rader? Before Rader obtained his present post as manager of the California Angels, he was a catcher with the Astros who, on a lark, used to hit balls around the locker room before a game, creating as much havoc as Alex Karras at Royal Oak. "He'd tee up a golf ball while guys would dive for cover in their lockers, behind trunks, and under the whirlpool," recalls a teammate, Larry Dierker. "Then he'd hit the ball, real hard, too, and it would ricochet around the room as the players prayed it wouldn't hit them."

Most big-time jocks use golf as a release, which, again, is not much different from the rest of us, who like to get out on the course to forget about the pressures of the job, the boss, money worries, the spouse, etc. Jocks fudge on their scores just as we do, and they cheat. At the Crosby Pro-Am, Cris Collingsworth of the Cincinnati Bengals testified that he was a twenty handicapper, and then went out and beat the pro he was playing with to lead the amateur field after the first round. At another tournament Steve DeBerg, the journeyman quarterback, hit what most people thought was a water shot, but DeBerg swore he found his ball next to the hazard. He hit his next shot onto the green, and somebody noticed that this ball had a red stripe on it. "Hey, man," said DeBerg, "I've been using a range ball all day." Sure, Steve.

The most famous jock golfer is Michael Jordan, whose day job is with the Chicago Bulls of the NBA. The world's greatest slam-dunk artist caused some comment a few years ago when he appeared on the cover of *Sports Illustrated* in his golf togs and announced his desire to play the PGA Tour after he got tired of making millions in basketball. This did not sit well with John Brodie, the former 49ers quarterback who's a fair-to-middling golfer on the geriatric circuit. "Michael Jordan has about as much chance of being a good professional golfer as I do of being a world-class basketball player," said Brodie. "That kind of talk insults me." Brodie is one of several ex-pros who've taken up golf as a kind of athletic second calling. Ralph Terry, the former New York Yankees pitcher, and ex-footballer Ed Whittenton, are two more. The three elder jocks are competitive, though hardly thriving, among their Ben-Gay brethren, but Brodie's resentment appears to stem not from professional jealousy, but from the implication that golf is an easy game that a person—even a person as gifted athletically as Jordan—can simply pick up in their late twenties and thirties and then have easy success with.

To Jordan's credit he never said this. What he said was: "When I get to the point where I can shoot consistently in the low seventies, I'd like to turn pro. I'm not saying I'm gonna win. I'm gonna try." Jordan isn't steadily in the low 70s yet, and you have to figure that he's going to hang around the round-ball game for a few years more and make sure that his bank account is well cushioned. But whatever Jordan does, you have to give him credit for a somewhat more progressive attitude than, say, Mychal Thompson of the Lakers. Asked what his handicap in golf was, Thompson laughed and said, "I'm black."

From Taft to Bush: A Gallery of Golfing Presidents

A favorite pastime of American presidents is to play golf, and a favorite pastime of the American people is to ridicule them while they're playing golf. It's a great country, isn't it?

The first dedicated golfer to become president was William Howard Taft, a member of the pioneering St. Andrew's Golf Club in New York State. Taft, a Republican, first took up the game in the late

1890s, and by the time he became president, in 1909, he had been playing well over a decade. Although, by his own admission, he wasn't very good at it. "I would, in respect to any other matter, feel very much discouraged at having attained in so long a time so little excellence," he said once. "But golf is different from other games. Pope's lines have a greater application to it than to any other sport I know: 'Hope springs eternal in the human breast.'"

But golf proved to be a liability for Taft as a politician. Theodore Roosevelt, who preceded Taft as president, advised his friend never to have his picture taken while playing golf. "It would seem incredible that anyone would care one way or the other about your playing golf," Roosevelt wrote to Taft during the latter's term in office. "But I have received hundreds of letters from the West protesting it. I myself play tennis, but that game is a little more familiar; besides you never saw a photograph of me playing tennis, I am careful about that; photographs of me on horseback, yes; tennis, no. And golf is fatal."

Unlike Roosevelt, who served two terms, Taft was turned out of office after only four years—a development, however, that cannot be blamed on golf, for his successor, Woodrow Wilson, was also mad about the game. Warren Harding, the next in the presidential line, was an avid player as well.

The most beloved golfing president ever was Dwight Eisenhower, and stories about his addiction to the game are legion. One day a visitor noticed the president with a bandage on his left wrist. The man asked what was wrong and Eisenhower said it was a mild arthritic condition. "Oh, I'm glad it's not serious," said the visitor. The president was taken aback. "Not serious?" he said. "I'll say it's serious. It means I can't play golf."

Eisenhower was a member of both the Royal and Ancient Golf Club of Scotland and Augusta National, where he played frequently during his presidency. On his orders, a putting green was installed on the White House lawn. After leaving office he became best of friends with Arnold Palmer, and the two men and their wives occasionally spent a social evening playing bridge together. A painting by Eisenhower hung in the Palmer household. On the evening of Arnold's thirty-seventh birthday, Mamie and Winnie cooked up a little surprise that involved Ike. Sitting at home reading the paper, Arnold was relaxing before dinner when the doorbell rang. He stood up to answer it and there, with a big grin on his face, was the man who liberated Europe from the Nazis. "Happy birthday, pro," said Eisenhower.

Ike loved golf to a fault, or so said his critics, who accused him of spending more time playing than he did running the country. During his reelection campaign in 1956, one bumpersticker read:

BEN HOGAN FOR PRESIDENT
IF WE'RE GOING TO HAVE A GOLFER, LET'S HAVE A GOOD ONE

A popular joke during Ike's time had him out on the golf course playing a round when all of a sudden he rushes up to the foursome ahead of him and asks if he and his partners could play through. "Sure," says one of the golfers in the party ahead, "but what's the hurry?" "New York was just bombed," says Ike.

(Not surprisingly, perhaps, a similar joke was told about George Bush after the Iraqi invasion of Kuwait in the summer of 1990 and the subsequent buildup of American forces in the Persian Gulf and Saudi Arabia. During this time Bush insisted on remaining on vacation and playing golf. But in the event a shooting war broke out while he was on the course, the Secret Service had strict orders to rush up to the foursome ahead and ask: "May the president play through?")

After Ike came Jack Kennedy, whose sporting tastes ran more to touch football and sailing, but who also played golf. But Kennedy was far more sensitive than Eisenhower about being photographed while golfing. Asked about this by a reporter, he replied, "It is true that my predecessor did not object as I do to pictures of one's golfing skill in action. But neither, on the other hand, did he ever bean a Secret Service man."

One suspects, though, that the savvy JFK avoided shots of him playing golf more for political reasons than for the sake of modesty. Associated as it is with the upper classes, golf can be a public relations nightmare for a politician wanting to present the image of being a man (or woman) of the people. Throw out the first pitch of the All-Star game, yes. Toss around the ole pigskin with the national championship college team, great. But show up on the grassy green fairways of a country club that denies admission to all but aging billionaire WASPS? Maybe we'd better rethink that one.

Jack Kennedy's successor, Lyndon Johnson, was not a golfer. Nor was Richard Nixon, although as with so many other aspects of his presidency and his life, he has tried to rewrite history, claiming in one of his recent books that he once broke 80. Lewis Grizzard could not sit still for that. "Hold it!" said Grizzard. "Who was keeping score, G. Gordon Liddy?"

Nixon once called golf "a waste of time," echoing the words of an earlier Republican president, the parsimonious Calvin Coolidge, who "did not see the sense in chasing a little white ball around a field." But if Nixon did not like to play much, he did, at least, enjoy tootling around in his golf cart quite a lot. According to one report, the horse-riding trails at Camp David were paved at Nixon's behest so that he could drive around the retreat in his cart. And in 1973, when visiting Soviet premier Leonid Brezhnev came a'calling in California, the president gave him a ride around his San Clemente estate in his golf cart. Brezhnev was supposedly so moved by this act of cordiality that tears came to his eyes.

Nixon's first vice president, Spiro T. Agnew, was even worse at golf than he was at being vice president, if that's possible. "Now there was a real wild man on the golf course," said Bob Hope, who played with Agnew as well as Eisenhower and many other prominent golfing politicians. "When Agnew yelled 'Fore!' you never knew if he was telling someone to get out of the way or if he was predicting how many spectators he would hit with his shot." At Hope's Desert Classic tournament Agnew hit the pro he was playing with, Doug Sanders, and three other spectators during one havoc-causing round.

Nixon's second vice president, Gerald Ford, who eventually succeeded him as president, had a reputation as being even wilder on a golf course than Spiro T. Aside from the many jokes about him as a crazy-driving golfer, Ford got embroiled in a minor controversy as president when a *Washington Post* reporter counted no fewer than thirty Secret Service men looking for a lost ball of his during a round of golf at a Virginia course. Some questioned whether this was a proper use of taxpayer funds—squads of highly trained Secret Service men looking for a ball they never found—and it helped teach Ford the value of discretion, politically speaking, when venturing out onto the golf links.

No one understands this better than our current vice president, Dan Quayle. Bar none, he is the most ridiculed golfing politician ever. When he was nominated for vice president in 1988, the media depicted him as a blue-eyed, blond-haired lightweight who had led a life of privilege—and proof of this was his background in golf. When he was a boy, his wealthy family moved to Scottsdale, Arizona, where they bought a home on a golf course. Young Dan played all the time, and when he and his parents returned to his native Indiana, he starred on his high school golf team and later at DePauw University, where he was an average student but the number one golfer. A spoiled rich kid from a country club family, the best connections that money could buy, a Republican *and* a golfer—it all added up, at least in the minds of Quayle's critics.

But it turned out that there was at least one thing they couldn't pin on him. During the '88 campaign it was reported that Quayle and a few other congressmen had gone to Florida on an all-expenses-paid junket in which the bosomy and blond lobbyist Paula Parkinson had sex with a few of the men from Washington. Not Quayle, though. "Anyone who knows Dan Quayle knows that given a choice between golf and sex, he will choose golf every time," his wife, Marilyn, said, and Parkinson herself testified that Quayle was innocent.

Since his first, rather bumpy introduction to national politics, Quayle has relaxed somewhat, consenting to play golf with the editors of various sports magazines doing feature stories on him. The vice president is an extremely competitive golfer who plays to a six and would probably be better than that if he had more time to devote to it. But outside of Washington, D.C., and a few other protected spots, he remains secretive about his game and fearful of that old golfing bugaboo: being photographed while in the act. "Every time we go on the road, they watch me," he told Rick Reilly. "They can't wait to catch me playing. So I never play on the road."

It is ironic that at a strategic moment in his presidency, Quayle's boss violated this rule and paid a dear political price for it. After the Iraqi invasion of Kuwait, George Bush was seen almost nightly on the television news fielding questions from reporters at the Cape Arundel Golf Club outside his Kennebunkport summer retreat. At first Bush clearly wanted to project a vacation-as-usual attitude and not alarm the American public unnecessarily with the threat of war. But as the days wore on and the military preparations picked up momentum, the pictures of the commander in chief still out on the golf course came to seem more and more out of place. "It's nice to see a president improving his golf game with the nation on the brink of war," gibed the columnist Gerald Nachman. "On the eve of Fort Sumter, they say, Lincoln was so nervous he was blowing routine six-foot putts."

But happily, that unfortunate experience with the media has not dissuaded Bush from continuing to play golf in a public way. Whatever else he accomplishes in his presidency, he has clearly put together, with Dan Quayle, the finest one-two golfing tandem in our nation's history.

Bush's ties to golf go back generations. His maternal grandfather, George Herbert Walker, was a president of the United States Golf Association and the founder of the Walker Cup, the biennial amateur-team matches pitting Great Britain and Ireland against the United States. Succeeding Walker as USGA president was Prescott Bush, George's father. Despite such impressive lineage, Bush claims he's never had a golf lesson in his life. A fast walker and speedy player, he has suffered in recent years from a wobbly putting game. But the adoption of an extralong putter favored by many seniors seems to have cured that, and he now shoots in the high 80s or thereabouts. Which is not bad considering all the other sports he plays, not to mention the other demands on his schedule.

Besides being an active player, Bush is a big fan of the professionals, too, and not long ago he invited Lee Trevino and Doug Sanders to the White House for dinner. After the meal Barbara Bush decided to take Millie, the family dog, out for an evening walk. The men joined her, and together they wandered across the White House lawn to the fence where some Australian tourists were peering in. Accompanied by the usual coterie of Secret Service agents, the group stopped to say hello to the visitors.

Mr. Bush began to introduce the golfers, but as he was doing so, one of the Australians interrupted him, saying, "You don't have to tell us who he is, Mr. President. In parts of Australia, Lee Trevino is more famous than you are."

And so it goes in the life of an American golfing president.

Gerald Ford, Headhunter

∽

First, hitting the ball.
Second, finding out where it went.

—Tom Watson, explaining how he helped
Gerald Ford with his golf game

The most famous headhunter in the annals of presidential golf is Gerald Ford. A fine natural athlete who played for the University of Michigan football team during his school days, Ford got his first taste of golf while caddying for his father at the old Masonic Golf Club in Grand Rapids, Michigan. He played off and on over the years during a distinguished political career, and after becoming president in 1974 following the resignation of Richard Nixon, he entered a charity golf tournament in Minneapolis in which, on the first hole, he beaned a spectator with his tee shot. From that point on, with an assist from his friend Bob Hope, his reputation on a golf course was set.

Hope has made a cottage industry out of Gerald Ford golf jokes. A sampling:

"There are over forty golf courses in Palm Springs, and nobody knows which one Ford is playing until after he hits his tee shot."

"It's not hard to find Gerry Ford on a golf course. Just follow the wounded."

"Ford's gallery doesn't come out to watch him play. They come to play chicken with his tee shots."

"Gerald Ford has made golf a contact sport."

"Ford's tee shots have created several new subdivisions."

"Ford is easy to spot on a golf course. He drives the cart with the Red Cross painted on top."

"Remember when Alan Shepard hit that golf ball on the moon?

Well, most people don't know that he found a golf ball when he was up there. Oh, yeah. It had Gerald Ford's name on it."

Ford, who plays to a handicap in the low to mid teens, was never as wild off the tee as Hope and others made him out to be. But he good-naturedly plays along with the gags, denying allegations that "during my last game I hit an eagle, a birdie, an elk, and a moose"; while adding, about Hope's game, "I know he'll shoot his age, even if he has to live to be one hundred and twenty-five to do it." The years have passed and the former president's name doesn't make it into the papers as much anymore, but his legend lives on. At a recent Seniors tournament in Napa, California, an approach shot by Don Bies hit a seventy-one-year-old woman in the gallery. She was not seriously hurt, but as a precaution she was taken to a nearby hospital for observation. As she was being lifted into the ambulance on a gurney, the woman sighed and said: "And it wasn't even President Ford."

Chi Chi

It's hard not to like somebody with the name of Chi Chi. Chi Chi is not a serious name. Chi Chi is the name of someone who dances nightly at the Kit-Kat Lounge and does intriguing things with tassels.

In this case, the Chi Chi belongs to Rodriguez, who belongs to golf. His given name is Juan, which in English is John, but that's far too plain a moniker for a person of his talents. Chi Chi is a personality and a star. Born in Puerto Rico and raised in the ghettos of San Juan, he does not fit the white-bread, country-club image that many people have of golfers.

Puerto Rico for Chi Chi is like Texas for Lee Trevino or the mountains of Virginia for Sam Snead. It's part of his identity. He can't escape it, not that he tries to or wants to. It's well known how Chi Chi raises money for hospitals and charities in Puerto Rico, and how his group—the Chi Chi Rodriguez Youth Foundation—gives underprivileged kids in Clearwater, Florida, a chance to play golf and work on a golf course and get their lives going on the right track.

But Chi Chi is long gone from the ghettos of San Juan where he grew up. He got out, and the way he got out was through golf. Near his house in San Juan was a country club where Chi Chi got his introduction to the game. There, he dreamed big dreams while earning a quarter for carrying a man's clubs around the course. You like rags-to-riches stories? Chi Chi has one of the best. "In my day you drank milk with a fork because you didn't want that glass of milk to run out," he says, joking about the poverty of his youth. "And when you had soup for lunch, you went outside and picked your teeth. You wanted the other guys to think you had meat."

As a kid Chi Chi crunched up a tin can and he had a ball. Then he ripped off a branch from a guava tree and he had a club. With his tin-can ball and tree-limb club, he began to imitate the players he saw at the country club. Later he graduated to real golf sticks and balls and took second in the Puerto Rican Open at a precocious seventeen. This was despite the opposition of his father, who told him that he'd never make it in golf because he was Puerto Rican and how many Puerto Rican golfers have you ever heard of? But Chi Chi was a tough hombre who proved his daddy wrong. He joined the pro tour in 1960, and although skinny as a 1-iron, he won eight tournaments over the years and became known as one of the best sand players in the game. "He has the greatest pair of hands in the golf business," said Gary Player, a man with a deft touch in the bunkers as well.

On a golf course, Chi Chi is outgoing and chipper and a crowd pleaser. Early in his career he got into trouble for hamming it up when he sank a birdie putt. He'd cover the hole with his hat, lifting the brim up a little and slyly peeking under to see if the ball was still there. Some of the humorless stiffs that golf is famous for objected, so as an alternative Chi Chi came up with a sword-fight routine with his putter that makes the galleries laugh yet doesn't offend.

Chi Chi's success in golf is a triumph of wit and guile over brawn. He laughs and makes merry, yet his jokes have a subtle, insurrectionary purpose. Jack Nicklaus hits a high, long ball, as is well known. Chi Chi hits 'em pretty well, too, but they tend to stay closer to the ground and roll farther after they land. On the right type of golf course Chi Chi in his prime could outdrive Nicklaus, but you'd never know it by his patter: "Oh, man," he would say to Nicklaus if they were paired together in a tournament, "I don't know how the golf ball can take a shot like you give it. Oh, man," Chi Chi would go on, his head drooping forlornly as he stepped up to the tee after Nicklaus, "did you see him smoke that ball? Unbelievable." Then Chi Chi would take his turn and pop a low-level screamer that after it stopped rolling would finish well beyond Jack's ball. That's the kind of psych that can hurt a person, although Nicklaus, who bested Chi Chi in a wonderful 1991 U.S. Senior Open playoff, seems to have survived it okay.

Chi Chi worked the angles on the regular tour, and now he's working them on the fifty-and-over set. After Trevino joined the Senior Tour and won three of the first four tournaments he entered, Chi Chi said, "Lee is in a different division. We don't even count him. If we finish second, that's like finishing first." Then, after Nicklaus (kicking and screaming) started playing with the seniors, Chi Chi ladled on some more: "When Jack and Lee show up, the rest of us are playing for third place." Meantime Chi Chi has continued to collect pin money on the circuit in addition to what he gets for playing exhibitions with corporate bigwigs, who pay small ransoms to hear him crack-wise and do that funny sword-fight thing with his putter.

Chi Chi moves through life like the happy and grateful man that he is. When Arnold Palmer caused a stir by saying that Senior Tour golfers should walk, not ride a cart, and if they didn't, they all might as wear petticoats, Chi Chi showed up the next day wearing a petticoat. Along with his straw hat and his putter dance, one of Chi Chi's trademarks is his humor, and down through the years he's come up with some good ones:

- "I'm playing like Tarzan—and scoring like Jane."
- "The best wood in most amateurs' bags is a pencil."
- "In the old days the goal was to become the head pro at a nice club. Now the idea is to buy the club."
- "I'd rather live rich and die poor. When you enjoy life and have peace of mind, you have everything. I'm a mental millionaire."
- At the Crosby tournament on the Monterey Peninsula some years back, Chi Chi faced a short but tough-to-read putt. "Which way do you think it will break?" he asked his caddie. "Toward the ocean, always toward the ocean," said the caddie. "Yeah," said Chi Chi, "but which ocean—the Atlantic or the Pacific?"

Looking back on his life, Chi Chi once told a reporter, "I always wanted to be the best golfer in the world, but Lee and Jack and Arnie were in the way. Oh well, at least I was the best Puerto Rican golfer in the world." As it turned out, that was pretty good in itself.

Mysterious Moe

Moe Norman was one strange cat. "Mysterious Moe," they called him, and for good reason. He slept in a car and refused to keep his money in a bank. He often wore the same clothes three or four days in a row, and he didn't seem to notice or mind that his shoes had holes in them or that his pants dragged along the ground as he walked.

Moe's idiosyncracies came out on a golf course as well. He would not have a caddy, even during a tournament when the other players had one. "The bag's not heavy," he explained. He drove off pyramid tees as well as soda-pop bottles. At one tournament he walked onto the first tee drinking a Coke, his favorite beverage. After he finished he set the bottle on the ground and used it for a tee. Peter Dobereiner says that Norman would often bet the resident pro that he could break the record at his golf course without having played or even seen it before. If, on a hole, the pro advised him that it was a drive and a 9-iron, Mysterious would hit the 9-iron first and then the driver—and birdie the hole.

Norman was strange, but good. Very, very good, if you believe the accounts of those who saw him play. "I do not know of any player who could strike a golf ball like Moe Norman, as far as hitting it solid, knowing the mechanics of the game, and knowing what he wanted to do with the ball," said Lee Trevino. Paul Azinger ran across Norman when Azinger was in college. He and his golf teammates were hitting balls at a practice range when Moe the Mysterious showed up and began hitting, too. "I couldn't believe what I was seeing," Azinger told a magazine interviewer. "I watched him hit drivers at the 250-yard sign and he never hit one more than ten yards left or right of the marker." In a demonstration Moe once hit six balls off the tee at a Florida golf course. All the balls landed within yards of each other, and two of the balls were touching.

Norman was born in Kitchener, Canada. He's still knocking around those parts, and he remains a cult figure of some standing in Canada as well as certain pro circles. His credits include two Canadian Amateur titles, two Canadian PGAs, and a handful of Canadian Senior PGAs in the past decade. But he never really made much of a go of it on the American circuit. He withdrew after two rounds at the 1956 Masters; all the spectators made him nervous. After winning the 1955 Canadian Amateur, which earned him his Masters invitation, he hid in the bushes by a river rather than receive his award from the tournament chairman.

Tour officials didn't know what to do with Moe. He played extremely fast—an admirable quality in almost all instances. But Norman's gait was so quick that the galleries could not keep up with him, and officials asked him to take a more circuitous path down the fairway to get to his ball. Though painfully shy around strangers, he was known to make side bets with the gallery on such subjects as how many times he could bounce a ball off the club face (his record was close to two hundred) or how many strokes it would take him to get out of a bunker hitting one-handed. In match play Moe would concede a ten-foot putt to his opponent before stepping up and draining a fifteen-footer himself. Three shots ahead on the final hole of a tournament, Moe had a dead-on putt. This was way too predictable, though, and he knocked the ball across the green into a bunker, whereupon he played out of the sand and sank the putt for the win. Despite the cloak of secrecy he wrapped around himself, a man such as Mysterious Moe cannot go unnoticed forever, and his hometown of Kitchener held a day in his honor a few years back. Bands played, people assembled, and the mayor stood poised to give him the key to the city. Moe never showed.

Hustler's Paradise

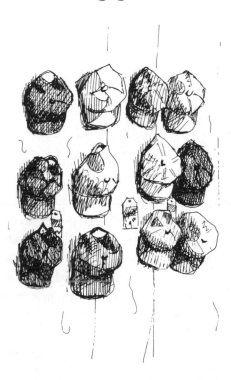

In its glory years in the 1950s and 1960s, Tenison Park in Dallas was the ultimate combination of two great American pastimes: golf and gambling. On an average day in, say, 1965, you could find more action at Tenison than at a horse track. You didn't just play golf at Tenison Park, you bet golf.

A long, rolling municipal course distinguished by the thousands of pecan trees almost everywhere in sight, Tenison attracted a whole bunch of characters you might normally expect to find on the wall of your post office. Nassau Nick, an ex-con who was once led off the course in handcuffs, the Fat Man, and the Redeemer were typical habitués of Tenison. The Redeemer used to dress in black like a preacher and hide in the pecan trees until he saw a foursome come by who were playing and making bets. Then he'd jump out and harangue the men for keeping company with the devil, or some such craziness. It was just a Tenison Park con. The Redeemer would somehow wiggle-waggle himself into the game and start making wagers of his own. The innocent foursome would not know that they were playing with a seasoned golf hustler, and by the end of the round their wallets would be lighter and the Redeemer's correspondingly heavier. And so it went.

Every golf course has more side bets going on than a Vegas casino, but it wasn't just penny-ante stuff at Tenison. The betting was long and strong. People knew about it and they expected it and they came there because of it. "It was the only golf course I've ever seen where the parking lot was filled with Cadillacs, jalopies, pickups, and beverage trucks," said one Tenison Park regular. It might also have been the only golf course where you could show up in a jalopy and drive away in a Caddy. Hundreds of dollars changed hands every day, and when the big shots came to play, the stakes went up a lot higher than that. On those days men packing guns made their appearance at Tenison, and they didn't work for the police.

Holdups took place on the course. Four gambling golfers were on the 8th hole when suddenly two men emerged from the trees. "Give us your money," said a stickup man. As soon as one of the golfers heard this, he quickly counted out ten one-hundred dollar bills and gave it to his partner. "Here," he said, "this is the thousand dollars I owe you. We're even."

That story sounds like a phony, but so does the name Titanic Thompson, and *he* existed in real life. Titanic was a golf-course hustler of legendary repute whose scams were known from coast to coast. His talents were such that he could not stay in any one place for long and had to travel from town to town, much like the circus. In the early 1960s—before the crackdown on gambling came and the place lost its wild-west flavor—he found his way to Tenison and immediately fell into the scene. Titanic was a player all right, one of the all-time best.

Nobody knows how Titanic got his name. One story has it that he was on board the *Titanic* at the time it hit that iceberg, but rather than go down with the ship he dressed up in women's clothes and climbed into a lifeboat to save his neck. This is, of course, preposterous, but so many of Titanic's doings are preposterous that it's impossible to ferret out the fact from the fiction.

He was tall and slim with blue eyes. He had a nice, easygoing personality, essential for a hustler. You don't want to come on too strong; otherwise you'll scare the pigeons away. Titanic could flip a Bicycle playing card and make it stick in a sliced watermelon fifteen feet away. You don't believe that? Wanna bet? One time in New York City, Titanic bet a man $5,000 that he could flip twelve cards out of a pack of fifty-two under a hotel door into a top hat turned upside down. Titanic and the man were outside the door in the hallway. There was a one-inch clearance under the door, and the top hat was on the other side. As Titanic did his flipping, an accomplice came up the fire escape from the room below, entered through the window that Titanic had left open for him, put the required number of cards in the hat, and slid out the window again. The pigeon never caught on, and Titanic and his friend flew south with an easy five grand.

"To be a winner, a man has to feel good about himself and know he has some kind of skillful advantage going in," said Mr. T, who always sought that advantage. He could play golf left-handed or right-handed. If he beat someone right-handed, he might say, "Hey, I'll give you a break. This time I'll play left-handed," and take some more of the guy's money. He might show up at a club in Florida looking pale and wan and complaining that he'd been so sick lately that he hadn't been able to play much golf. This would engender some action of a pecuniary nature, to which the weakened Titanic would be forced to acquiesce. Naturally he had been practicing like a madman all winter long in a long-sleeve shirt, hat, and gloves, and he'd walk away with the cash.

Driving into town with a friend, Titanic might happen to notice a mileage marker that read DALLAS: 20 MILES. Titanic would then casually say to the driver that he thought it was more like seventeen, causing a polite disagreement and prompting a wager. The driver would not have known that Titanic had gone out the day before and moved the mileage marker in closer to town by three miles.

You might stumble upon Titanic eating from a bag of walnuts. As you sat and chatted real friendly like with him, he might offer you a walnut or two as he continued to munch. When he got to the last nut in the bag, he'd say, "I bet I can throw this walnut over that clubhouse over there," to which you might respond, "Titanic, I believe you have been temporarily relieved of your senses. No human being can throw a walnut that far." After the money was put down, Titanic would wind up and throw that lead-filled walnut over the clubhouse.

One of his most inspired tricks on a golf course involved putting. He'd put a hose down on a green that had just been watered. The next day, when they mowed the green, the place where the hose had been left formed a narrow trough in the grass. When Titanic and his golfing partners came to this green he'd bet that he could sink, oh, say, three of five putts from thirty feet. And sure enough, Titanic would send those balls sailing straight down the trough into the hole.

Titanic didn't like having his photograph taken; he didn't want his face to be too well known. He often worked in teams. He might pay a younger guy to show up at a club, find out who the players were, and report back to him. When Titanic paid a visit a few days later, he had all the information he needed. Or he might set up games for his caddie and bet on him. His caddies were invariably ringers. Lee Elder, the former PGA pro and current Senior player, caddied for Titanic. So did the fiery half-Indian Ky Laffoon. But Titanic's greatest find was the one that got away. By the time he came to

Tenison Park, Titanic was getting on in years and wanted to hook up with somebody who would do the playing while he managed the betting. They'd go around the country playing at the different courses and make a pile of money together. He found the hotshot he was looking for at Tenison, but unfortunately for Ti, this young man had other ideas for himself and declined the offer. His name: Lee Trevino.

Super Mex

God is a Mexican.

—Lee Trevino

Dinah Shore has said that if she had her pick of three partners to play a round of golf with, one of them would be Lee Trevino. (The other two would be Amy Alcott, the woman's pro, and the actor Robert Wagner.) That's about right. If asked which big-name golfer they'd enjoy having as a partner, most people would probably put Trevino's name at the top of the list, too.

And why not? He's talkative, he's funny, and he plays wonderful golf even as he has turned the corner on fifty and moved into competition with "the roundbellies" of the Senior Tour, as he calls them. Labeling himself Super Mex, Trevino first made headlines in 1968 with his wholly unexpected U.S. Open triumph. Much of what he has done and said since then has been equally unexpected, yet wholly delightful. Some examples:

- Prior to the start of the British Open one year Trevino was attending a gala banquet in which the British, as is their custom, were making repeated toasts to the royal family.

  "To the queen!" said one, hoisting a glass.

  "To the prince of Wales!" said another.

  So Trevino stood up and said, "To Paul Revere!"

- At another British Open the rough was practically cornstalk high, according to Trevino. "On one hole we put my bag down to look for a lost ball. We found the ball but lost the bag." After coming in 1-under for a tournament, he explained how he did it: "I was one under a tree, one under a bush, one under the water."

- So many of his lines are keepers: "The two things that don't last for long are pros putting for bogeys and dogs chasing cars." Or his famous explanation for why he prefers the fade over the hook: "You can talk to a fade. But a hook won't listen."

- Trevino, the Texas-born son of a Mexican gravedigger, has always poked fun at his roots. "I always thought manual labor was a Mexican," he is fond of saying. "If it wasn't for golf, I don't know what I'd be doing," he adds. "If my IQ had been two points lower, I'd have been a plant somewhere." After his 1968 Open win, he remarked, "As soon as I win some more money, I'll be a Spaniard instead of a Mexican." His fellow pros have gone along with the gag. The year after Trevino pulled his surprise at Oak Hill, Orville Moody, an unknown ex-army-sergeant, won the U.S. Open. "What does it matter who Orville Moody is?" cracked Dave Marr. "At least he brought the title back to America."

- Flushed with his victory at Oak Hill and the $30,000 in prize money, Trevino said, "I may buy the Alamo and give it back to Mexico." The remark got such a reaction that he had to make a tour of the historic battle site. "Well, I'm not gonna buy it after all," he said after his visit. "It doesn't have indoor plumbing."

- Despite the jokes, Trevino, who still does not belong to a private club, has always been sensitive about his upbringing. His gibes at the Masters over the years may not be solely due to his complaints about the layout of the Augusta National course. Trevino won the 1984 PGA at Shoal Creek Country Club in Birmingham, Alabama. Until the controversy surrounding the 1990 PGA, which forced it to change its admission policies and admit an honorary black member, Shoal Creek was an all-white establishment in the heart of Dixie. Trevino's caddie for the 1984 event was a chunky black man named Herman Mitchell. As they walked down the fairway during a round, a man in the gallery shouted, "Hey, Lee, what do you feed your caddie?"

"Rednecks," said Lee, not missing a beat. "And he's hungry."

- Trevino has also made an occasional wife joke or two. His third wife happened to have the same name—Claudia—as his second wife. "It couldn't have worked out more perfectly," said Lee. "I didn't even have to change the initials on the towels or sheets." His wife was hurt by the remark and Lee later apologized for it, but he went on to tell the press that he and Claudia had just moved five hundred miles to a new home and the funny thing was, his wife still had the same milkman.

Various people have observed that the off-stage Trevino is a far more private and guarded individual than his public persona—that he has a sharpness to his personality and jokes, an edge. "He's much more highly strung than people imagine," notes the golfer Tony Jacklin. Tom Boswell, who covers golf for the *Washington Post*, writes: "[Trevino is] the funniest man in golf and perhaps the most bitter. His humor—usually about class, race, sex, or physical appearance— is a sword with which he entertains the world while also keeping it at bay. He'll cut you off at the knees." Larry Dorman, another writer-cum-psychologist, observes, "This is a complex man. He is at once elusive and engaging, churlish and pleasant. . . . Had he been a boxer instead of a golfer, he would not have been hit very often."

The analogy with boxing is apt, for Trevino has made the comparison many times himself. "Golf is like fighting," he has been quoted as saying. In describing his rivalry with Nicklaus in a magazine interview, Trevino used these words: "A guy can beat the hell out of you, but you keep getting up. Finally the guy says, 'Man, when is this guy going to lie down?' I know there were times Jack felt like that against me."

Trevino keeps getting up; he's no quitter. That may be why we like him and why we keep cheering for him—despite, or perhaps because of, those rough edges. How many other members of the pampered pro set used to hustle golf games with a Dr Pepper bottle? Trevino would use one of those thick thirty-two ounce Dr Pepper bottles—they don't make them anymore—while his mark would play with all the regulation clubs. Lee shot pars and birdies with that bottle and claims he never lost a bet with it. After he became famous, the soft-drink company found out about his unusual use of their product and signed him to a mouth-watering endorsement contract.

In his Dr Pepper days, Trevino played at Tenison Park in Dallas—the world-renowned home of golf hustlers, gamblers, and miscreants of all types—while working at a nearby driving range and 9-hole pitch 'n' putt. He joined the Marines as a teenager and following his discharge, came to Dallas in the summer of 1961. He was twenty-one and ambitious in a golfing way. He used to hit two thousand balls a day. Some mornings he would be at Tenison so early that only the mosquitoes were up to greet him. He packed his arms and legs with creek mud to avoid getting bit and carried his bag across his back or slung over his shoulder like a rifle. His bag had a gaping hole in the bottom, and if he had carried it the usual way, the clubs would have fallen out.

"You don't know what pressure is until you play for five bucks with two in your pocket," Trevino has said, recalling his days at Tenison Park and later, Horizon Hills in El Paso. Trevino had foolishly quit his job at Hardy's Driving Range, upset that his employer wouldn't sign his Class-A PGA card that would've given him a shot at the Tour. Broke and out of work, he packed up their belongings in a U-Haul and moved his wife and baby daughter to El Paso, where he had the promise of a job. Trevino had fifty dollars in his pocket when he arrived, which may not sound like much, but he always had the hustler's God-given ability to parlay a little into a lot. Cotton farmers liked to play—and gamble—at Horizon Hills, and Lee was only too happy to oblige them on both accounts.

But Trevino made his gambling at golf pay double. Not only did he use it to help support himself and his family, it served as a means of preparation for his ultimate goal: the big PGA tamale. He'd play against friends, who'd use the ladies' tees while he hit from the championship tees. He'd play their best ball, with money on the line. "If I didn't shoot sixty-six, I'd lose," said Trevino. They made up betting games. One was a five-dollar Nassau in which Trevino had to miss every green on his second shot in order to chip on his third. The unconventional training made for an unconventional golfer— "Just figure out a way to get it in the hole, no matter what it looks like" was his philosophy—but the results are there for all to see. Fifth at the Open in 1967, the big win the next year. That tremendous winning string in 1971: the U.S., Canadian, and British Opens, all within the span of a month. His stare-him-down-and-make-him-blink showdowns with Nicklaus, and now, his successes on the Senior Tour.

"Nobody taught me to play," Trevino once told Tom Callahan. "Nobody paid my way. I don't want to sound like I have a chip on my shoulder, but when you have done something yourself—it's a very sweet feeling, a very proud feeling." Nobody has more reason to feel proud of himself than Lee Trevino, but it's not quite accurate to say he did it all by himself. During the week of the 1968 Open, the tournament that started everything for him, he stayed with a family in Rochester. He was twenty-eight, and unknown. When he went to the course to practice, nobody paid any attention to him. "Every afternoon I sat in a golf cart for two or three hours and drank beer," he recalled, laughing. "No one ever stopped to say hello. I think they thought I was the cart boy." The family he stayed with had a four-year-old girl who seemed a little frightened of him. To get on her good side Trevino took her into the backyard to look for four-leaf clovers. They got on their hands and knees and started combing through the grass. The girl couldn't find any, but her new friend wouldn't give up, and in a matter of time he was calling out to her, grinning from ear to ear, holding a lucky clover delicately between his thumb and forefinger. By Sunday the former muni-park hustler would be the national champion and begin a ride on a lucky streak that hasn't stopped yet.

Rivalry II
(Nicklaus-Trevino)

The year was 1972 and Jack Nicklaus was riding a wave. He had won the Masters and U.S. Open and was now taking aim at the third leg of the Grand Slam, the British Open. Everything was coming together. Ridiculed for years about his weight and appearance, the Golden Bear had finally decided to trim down after the 1969 Ryder Cup matches, where he had played thirty-six holes in a day and for the first time on a golf course, felt tired and listless. This was unacceptable to him, and in typically Nicklausian manner he set about to lose some pounds. Eating mainly chicken and fish, with plenty of vegetables and five citrus fruits a day, he shed thirty pounds in five weeks, dropping from 210 to 180. In addition, Nicklaus got rid of his equally ridiculed crew cut, substituting a more contemporary hairstyle.

These changes coincided with a time of reevaluation and tragedy in Nicklaus's life. His father fell ill with cancer in late 1969 and died the following year. Jack, who had not won a major tournament in two years, felt as if he had let his dad down in the last year of his life. This made him even more determined to get back on top of the golf world, and when Doug Sanders let him in the door with a missed putt on the final green of the 1970 British Open at St. Andrews, Nicklaus had his chance. He beat Sanders in a playoff and in jubilation, hurled his putter into the air on the 18th green. When it came down, it nearly hit Sanders in the head, but the more important message sent by that up-flung club was that Jack was back.

Tom Weiskopf tells a story about Nicklaus needing to sink a ten-foot putt to stay in the lead of a tournament. After studying the break for a long time, Nicklaus putted and sent the ball straight for the hole. But the ball stopped right at the rim and refused to go in. "I don't care if the ball didn't drop," said Nicklaus firmly. "I hit it in the hole."

Jack's self-confidence, which has never suffered from under-nourishment, got a big boost after St. Andrews. He had won a major again, and he had done it in the ancestral home of golf. The next year he won the PGA and took second at the U.S. Open and the Masters (the latter in a tie with Johnny Miller). The ball was not dropping in every major tournament Jack played, but he was most assuredly hitting it into the hole. By 1972, as Nicklaus himself has noted, the press was asking not whether Jack would win the Grand Slam, but when. And after Nicklaus marched through Augusta National and then Pebble Beach at the National Open, the dream of a modern Slam in a single year seemed entirely within his reach.

And if it hadn't been stolen away by a crazy chip shot from out of nowhere, he might have done it, too.

The chip was performed—or perpetrated, if you like—by Lee Trevino, that well-known confidence man and consummate golf hustler. Some might regard "hustler" as a derogatory term, but not when applied to the man who had hustled himself the 1968 U.S. Open and for the next six years played a level of golf only Nicklaus and a few others in the past four or five centuries can match. A hustler plays people as much as he plays the game, and this may have been why Trevino was so successful against Nicklaus. He didn't win all the time in the major championships against Nicklaus, but he played him no worse than even, which is a heckuva lot better than most people can claim.

"Jack brought out the best in me every time," Trevino told an interviewer once. "I would match him, shot for shot. And nothing pleased me more. I could care less about anybody else in the field. I didn't even care who was leading the tournament, as long as I'd beat him when we were paired together."

When Trevino won the 1968 Open, Nicklaus finished second. But Super Mex snuck up on everybody that year. A more famous duel took place in 1971 at the U.S. Open at Merion, where they tied after four rounds, and Trevino, in a prank, teased Jack with a rubber snake before whipping him in an 18-hole playoff, 68 to 71. More from Trevino: "I know that Nicklaus has always been scared of me. I knew it at Merion. He looked nervous at Merion. I used to go up to him and just poke him with my finger like it carried an electric shock. Then I'd say, 'That's all I got to do.' "

The public warmed to the Nicklaus-Trevino confrontations, as it had to the earlier Nicklaus-Palmer rivalry, now cooled since Palmer had fallen off as a major tournament player. They saw in the Nicklaus-Trevino duel not just the possibilities for great golf, but a clash of cultures, personalities, style. Nicklaus was blond and aloof; Trevino, a Hispanic, was outgoing and fun and always a good quote for the newspaper guys. Nicklaus, sired in the country club tradition, hit a high, classic ball and loved the irons. Many said he was the greatest of all time, greater even than the great Bobby Jones, whose records Nicklaus was chasing. Trevino, on the other hand, played his early golf on municipal courses, hitting golf balls with Dr Pepper bottles and hustling strangers for rent money in Dallas and El Paso. His best club was the wedge. Unlike Nicklaus he looked awkward when he swung, but as with his rival, the ball always seemed to end up exactly as he planned.

By the time the British Open rolled around, in Muirfield, Scotland, Trevino was as voluble as ever. "I didn't come to Scotland to help Nicklaus win any Grand Slam," he said. "If I played golf with my wife, I'd try to beat the daylights out of her." The British press was calling it "the Grand Slam Open," but Trevino and the Englishman Tony Jacklin weren't having any of it. At the end of three rounds Trevino was the leader, a stroke up on Jacklin and six strokes up on Nicklaus, who seemed oddly lethargic, off his game. What was wrong? the press asked. Was he asleep?

On Sunday, the Bear awoke. Troubled by a stiff neck earlier in the tournament and accused of being too conservative in his play, Nicklaus began to inflict a major hurt on the Muirfield golf course. He birdied 2, 3, 5, 9, and 10 and pounded the tournament into a dramatic new shape. When Trevino and Jacklin, who were paired together and playing behind Nicklaus, stepped up to the first tee, Trevino said, "Jack might catch one of us, but he won't catch both of us." By the time they reached the 9th tee Jack had caught and passed them both. After playing a 3-wood on 9 for each of the past three days, Trevino realized that the earth was shifting underneath him and he had to act. "Gimme a driver," he told his caddie. "We've got to make something happen." And he did. He hit a killer drive and eagled the hole. Amazingly, Jacklin, looking for his second British Open title, matched Trevino with an eagle of his own.

"That'll give Jack something to think about," Trevino joked as they turned to go to the next hole. A moment later a roar went up on 11. Jack had just sunk another birdie putt. "I think the man just gave us something to think about," said Trevino.

In the end, it came down to this: Nicklaus missed what was possible, Trevino made what was improbable, and Trevino won. After his birdie on 11, Nicklaus missed makable birdie putts on the next four holes, and on the 16th, a six-foot putt for par did everything but go in and he bogeyed. Nicklaus ended with a 66 and 279—one stroke more than he figured he needed to win. As it happened, Nicklaus was right, but only because of one last trick from a man who had apparently run out of them. On 17, Trevino put his third shot into the rough thirty yards from the green and tossed his club in disgust. His next shot—a chip, normally a Trevino strong point —shot across the green into thick grass. "I had the impression that Lee had given up," said Jacklin, and the buzz in the press tent where Nicklaus was watching on television was that Trevino was blowing sky-high. But blow he did not. Trevino, who later admitted that he had given up on the shot, took a whack at it with his 9-iron, and in the Miracle of Muirfield, the ball jumped into the cup. Super Mex had saved par, while Jacklin, who was on the green in three and sixteen feet away from a birdie and the lead, three-putted the hole. Jacklin was out of it and Trevino only a par away on 18 from his second straight British Open title and equally sweet, beating Nicklaus. He got the par.

"Golf can be a heartbreaking game," Nicklaus would write later, "and this was my No. 1 heartbreaker." Winning at Muirfield would've made Nicklaus the first since Hogan to win the U.S. and British Opens and the Masters in the same year. With the PGA coming later in the summer, it would've given him a shot at the modern Grand Slam, a feat that has yet to be accomplished. Bobby Jones won the old Grand Slam—the U.S. and British Opens and the British and U.S. Amateurs—in 1930. What's more, a win at Muirfield would've given Nicklaus his fourteenth major title, surpassing Jones's mark of thirteen. Jack had to wait another year until he got big No. 14. All these things could have happened but did not, and they did not because of an impossible-to-figure golfer who holed shots from off the green not one, not two, not three, but four times during the tournament. "I'll always believe I played the course the right way and just didn't play well," Nicklaus said in wonderment afterward. "But what can I do about a guy who holes it out of bunkers and across greens?" It was a question for which there was no ready answer.

Fifty-nine

All golfers hope to get into a good, hot groove when they play, but as long as you live, it's safe to say you will never get into a groove like the one Al Geiberger got into that day in Memphis. His drives shot off like bullets. His high, lazy approaches surveyed the green from above and parachuted softly down next to the pin. And his putts—man, his putts! That ball had eyes.

Al Geiberger's 59 at the 1977 Danny Thomas Classic was not the greatest round of tournament golf ever, not by a long shot. From a historical standpoint, the greatest rounds must take place at U.S. Opens or the Masters, not at tournaments named after large-nosed television stars.

Nonetheless, there it is . . . 59! Several people have shot 60 at PGA events over the years, but only Geiberger has broken the barrier and gotten into the 50s. He did it on Friday, June 10, 1977, at the 7,249-yard, par-72 Colonial Country Club. Due to the tournament scheduling, he started on the 10th hole and played through 18, then came back to 1 and finished on 9. His round went like this: eagle, birdie, birdie, par, par, birdie, birdie, par, birdie. Second nine: birdie, par, birdie, par, par, birdie, birdie, birdie, birdie. He birdied or eagled twelve of the eighteen holes. It's the kind of round you don't even dream about—it's too far out there, science fiction stuff.

"When I'm playing well sometimes it's as if my eyes change," said Jane Blalock, the touring pro. "I'm a totally different human being. I don't hear anybody, I don't see anybody, nothing bothers me." This must have been the way Geiberger felt when he was working the round of his life. He knew he had something going after the front nine; he couldn't remember the last time he had had a 30, much less a 29. But Geiberger resisted the urge to pull back and play it safe. He kept zeroing in on that pin, and amazingly, he kept hitting it.

Geiberger's life off the course has been marked by tragedy and reversals of fortune. Now a member of the Senior Tour, he has been divorced twice and undergone stomach and knee surgeries. His father died the year before his 59, and in 1988, he suffered the loss of his two-year-old son. But for one day in 1977, the lanky, six-foot-two Californian got as close to perfection on a golf course as anybody ever has.

Word of Geiberger's hot round spread quickly among the gallery. His threesome started out with only a handful of spectators, but by the 9th hole the crowd had snowballed. By the end it seemed as if there were no other spectators anywhere on the course; they were all watching Al. After his birdie on the 15th, the crowd, realizing what was at stake, began to shout: "Fifty-nine! Fifty-nine! Fifty-nine!" But the growing excitement and clamor didn't bother the man at the center of it. He was calm and eerily confident.

On the par-5 7th hole (his 16th), Geiberger stroked a nine-foot birdie putt that he didn't even need to see go in. He turned his back on it and waited for the crowd reaction to tell him if it dropped or not (it did). Geiberger putted like that all day. He took only twenty-three putts. Dave Stockton, one of his playing partners, said that the cup could have been the size of a cocktail glass and it wouldn't have mattered. Every one of Geiberger's putts went straight into the center of the hole.

But it wasn't just his putting. Inexplicably, every aspect of Geiberger's game was in a state of grace. His drives were consistently fifteen to twenty yards longer than normal. And when he closed out his run of four straight birdies on the four finishing holes and got that curiosity piece of a score, the ball he picked out of the hole was the only ball he had played the entire day.

A footnote. Asked later to explain the secret of his magical round, Geiberger said, "A great round of golf is a lot like a terrible round. You drift into a zone, and it's hard to break out of it." Two weeks after his 59 he entered the Western Open in Chicago and shot an 80. Golf giveth, and golf taketh away.

The Magic of a Hole in One

There are two reasons for making a hole in one.
The first is that it is immensely laborsaving.

—*H. I. Phillips*

The second thing to realize about a hole in one is that it is a piece of magic, like a rabbit pulled from a magician's hat. A truly amazing event that cannot happen but somehow quite frequently does. A hole in one is a wonder to see, and an even greater wonder to do. It is an expression of sporting perfection, yet it is not the exclusive preserve of the experts; the very worst golfers can get one, too. A hole in one is both elitist and democratic. Only a rare few can play in the major leagues or run for a touchdown; but any old duffer, no better than you or I, can make a one.

A hole in one is noteworthy; it demands comment. Even nongolfers wake up to it: "Hey, he hit a hole in one!" A wire story on a tournament reports the scores, names the leaders, tells the events of the day. At the bottom of the story it notes that Mr. So-and-so, who made par on the round, hit a hole in one on the 183-yard 5th. He used a 6-iron, the story dutifully reports. There's a glint of mystery, the Cheshire Cat's smile, in a hole in one. People want to know how it happened—who did it, what club was used—in order to share in the mystery, to see the smile before it disappears again.

No one expects to make a hole in one; it just happens. Three days after he won his third U.S. Open, Hale Irwin hit an ace in a tournament. Irwin was on a hot streak; his ace was another manifestation of that streak. In the 1989 Open four pros hit aces on the par-3, 167-yard 6th hole at Oak Hill. "Other than winning one, that's the greatest feeling I've ever had at an Open," said Jerry Pate, one of the lucky four to do it. This was an improbable occurrence—four aces on the same day in a high-stakes tournament—but there is always an element of improbability to a hole in one. It's an everyday miracle, the improbable made routine.

Curtis Strange made a hole in one on the difficult 12th at the 1988 Masters and then, for reasons even he couldn't quite explain, threw the ball into the water, never to be found again. What'd you do that for, Curtis? A hole-in-one ball belongs on the mantle, mounted on brass. When you get a hole in one you get your name in the local paper; *Golf Digest* sends you a certificate that you frame and put on your wall. You call your relatives, tell your friends (and bore them to tears with the story), and most important, you buy drinks all around after you do it. Bing Crosby hit a famous ace at the 16th at Cypress Point and said, "By the time I got back to the bar there were members there who hadn't been to the club in years." A hole in one always draws a crowd, even if you're not interested in a free drink; the dream of making an ace is one of the ties that bind the community of golf.

The pros make holes in one, but they really belong to the ordinary players, who can, rightfully, claim that on that one hole they hit a shot as well as it could have been hit. Bob Jones or Nicklaus or Arnold Palmer could not have done it better. An ace can only be duplicated, never surpassed. Nor can it be dismissed as simply a freak event. Holes in one occur too often for that.

A hole-in-one story always ends the same: ball in cup. But the stories of how they occur, how golfers beat the odds, are endless. And every year there are new stories. A husband and a wife each hit an ace on the same hole while playing together in a foursome. An eight-year-old boy knocks down a one in only his second round of golf. A Connecticut retiree hits an ace in 1930 with a wood-shafted mashie and then waits forty-seven years before he does it again (without the mashie). A blind Jacksonville, Florida, woman hits back-to back aces on the same hole on successive days; her triumph is reported around the country. Some lucky stiff hits two aces in the same round. A pregnant Oklahoma woman hits a 5-wood into the hole with a single stroke; hours later she's in the delivery room giving birth. A Canadian man hits two aces on different courses while playing two rounds in the same day. A Californian hits a ball that gets wrapped up in the flag and then drops into the hole. A young Japanese man plays golf on his wedding day and hits a one; the hotel where he's staying picks up his room tab. These fortunate souls all belong to a select yet nonexclusive golfing society, open to the great, the near-great, the not-great, and the merely lucky. They did it! They hit a hole in one!

Aces are always a surprise, sometimes even after you hit one. You hit it, lose track of the ball, search for it, give up, then discover it . . . *in the hole*. It is a revelation that does not unfold itself immediately—rather, in stages, like the petals of a flower opening toward the sun.

In the rest of our lives perfection is out of reach, an impossible dream; but on a par-3 hole with the wind blowing right, perfection is only an iron away. Somehow, this seems fitting—that golf, the most demanding and unyielding of sporting disciplines, should release its fingers from our throats now and then and let us breathe a little. There's a story about an Olympic Club bartender who didn't play golf or even watch it, but he got tired of hearing his customers complain about how hard it was. So one day he strolled out to the 8th green in time to see a golfer knock down a hole in one. "Hell," said the bartender, "what's so hard about this game? It looks easy to me." That's right. Golf *is* easy. Just ask anybody who's just hit a hole in one.

Swing Keys, and the Endless Search for Golf Wisdom

People who argue whether golf is a sport or a game are missing the point; it is neither. Golf is a metaphysical exercise. Golfers chase after enlightenment as much as they do for lost balls. They are always looking for that one piece of advice, that one kernel of wisdom that will somehow transform their game and lift it onto a higher plane, or at least shave a few strokes and get them under 120. A golfer will consult with anyone, including a stranger passing on the street, if he thinks that person can help him with his game.

"Golf is assuredly a mystifying game," said Bobby Jones, a man who was mystified less than most. "It would seem that if a person has hit a golf ball correctly a thousand times, he should be able to duplicate the performance almost at will. But such is certainly not the case." No, it is decidedly not the case, and golfers hardly need to be reminded of it. This is the reason for their ceaseless quest. This is why they are searching: to find an answer to the mystery.

Golfers read, watch, and listen voraciously, all with the aim of discovering that ever-elusive swing "key" that will unlock the gates of the green kingdom. A swing key is a mantra, really. Ommmmmm. A thought or a word or a phrase that enables you to click into a good rhythm and hit the ball according to your deepest desires. Swing keys are serious business. It is well documented that the pros rely on them, too. They get into bad habits, and when this happens, they consult their swing-key gurus, men who reside in Florida and live like princes off their book and video royalty income.

Even if you have the money to afford one of these gurus, choosing the right one can be a real dilemma. Golf teachers, like fish, swim in schools, and over the years the theoreticians of the various schools have clashed with one another in mighty debate. One school says right, the other school says left, and every now and then a theory will arise that nobody should pay attention to but everyone does. Which way should the golfing pilgrim turn? It's not easy to say.

One of the leading schools of golf thought might be labeled "the Naturalists." They believe in trusting your native instincts. Their greatest exponent was Sam Snead ("Playing golf is like eating. It's something which has to come naturally"), but there are many other advocates as well. "If a five-year-old child can learn to swing, there is no reason on earth why you cannot," wrote Ernest Jones in his Naturalist manifesto, *Swing the Clubhead*. "All you need to do is repeat the action of that child. Her mind was not cluttered by the countless don'ts that fill the air wherever people talk golf. She merely took the club as it should be taken, in her two hands, and did with it what comes naturally. She swung."

Putting aside any resentment you might feel in being compared to a five-year-old girl (and unfavorably at that), any objective seeker of golf truth must see great merit in the view of Jones and his ("The more you know, the worse you score"—Forrest Fezler) disciples.

And yet—and this is why wisdom, in golf, is so elusive—there are many people who think the Naturalists have got it dead wrong.

"Reverse every natural instinct you have and do just the opposite of what you are inclined to do and you will probably come very close to having a perfect golf swing," said Ben Hogan, a doctrinaire Anti-Naturalist. In the Anti-Naturalist School, all that "let the child in you emerge" stuff is dismissed as so much Pablum. The Anti-Naturalists believe there are no shortcuts to golf enlightenment; that it comes only through a strict adherence to technique, self-discipline, and hard work. "The more I practice, the luckier I get," said Gary Player, in

a perfect expostulation of the Anti-Naturalist credo that all good things come to those who work for them. And certainly, there can be no denying that many good things came to Player in his time.

But will good things happen to everybody if they work like dogs at the game? Not hardly. "Golf is a game where guts, stick-to-itiveness, and blind devotion will get you absolutely nothing but an ulcer," said Tommy Bolt, who helped relieve his potential gastrointestinal problems by hurling and breaking his clubs. This, however, is not recommended.

A chief tenet of Anti-Naturalist theory is the avoidance of mistakes on a golf course. "The difference between the winner and the near-winner is the ability on the part of the successful contestant to be ever on the lookout against himself," said the Englishman J. H. Taylor, one of the top three golfers in the world at the turn of the century despite himself. By being on the lookout against himself, a golfer plays a canny kind of tactical game—minimizing his mistakes while waiting for the other person to screw up. "Golf is not a game of great shots," said Phil Rodgers, a respected golf teacher. "It's a game of great misses." Adds Jack Nicklaus, who surely knows whereof he speaks: "The game of golf is not how many good shots you hit, it's how few bad shots you hit."

Avoid blowups, limit your bad shots, use wise course management. Common sense, yes. But the keys to the kingdom? Not so fast. There are those who say that avoiding mistakes is too negative an outlook. It gets a person thinking too much ("The mind messes up more shots than the body," sayeth the aforementioned Mr. Bolt) and not concentrating on the thing itself—hitting that tater. Timothy Gallwey, the "inner game" guru, believes that golf should be played with "less ego interference" and that people should get "out of the trying mode and into an awareness mode." In other words, don't try to get the ball out of the trap; just get it out. This sounds a little reminiscent of the famous "Let the club swing you" theory of golf, which may have made sense to some people but probably confused a lot more. Confusion being one of the chief hallmarks of golf theory, this points to one of the dangers faced by the average golfer, a danger faced as far back as the late 1800s when Sir Walter Simpson was writing. "The average golfer must be allowed to theorize to some extent," said Simpson in *The Art of Golf*. "On the other hand, if he does not recognize hitting the ball as his main recreation, he becomes so bad a player that he nearly gives it up." Paralysis by analysis, and all that.

So you should think about your game, but not so much that it gets in the way of your game. And you should or should not trust your instincts, depending on what your instincts tell you. But whatever you do, almost everyone agrees that you shouldn't believe everything you read, including this. "A great deal of what is said and written about golf is wrong," said Joe Dante, and he's right. Or wrong, depending on your view of Dante.

"It's all in the head," a golfer will tell you, tapping his skull sagely. Indeed it is, and admittedly that's a big part of the problem. Golf is such a thinking game, you can never stray too far from the mental side of the game. There's no avoiding it despite what the instinctualists want you to think.

But, say some swing gurus, through the practice of visualization the mind need not be your enemy; it can be your friend. As the great Nicklaus counsels, before each shot see a "movie" in your mind of how you want that shot to go, and maybe, just maybe, your shot will go according to script. The story is told of an American military officer who was captured by the Viet Cong during the Vietnam War and placed in solitary confinement for five years. To keep himself sane, he played a round of golf every day in his head. He went into such detail that it took him hours to play an imaginary round. Then, after the end of the war and his release from prison, he returned to the U.S. and played a game of golf for real, his first time in years and years. Although he had broken 90 only a few times before, all this positive visualization paid off in a major way. He shot a 74.

This is a wonderful story, but it seems a bit drastic to even the most ardent swing-key searcher. There have to be simpler solutions.

"Play happy," Nancy Lopez's dad told her, and that certainly seems a more fun approach to the game than five years in solitary confinement. Be sure to stop and smell the roses, and the inner contentment you feel will enable you to reach your peak. Says Peter Thomson: "Your mind works the best when you're happiest."

But does it really? Curtis Strange, who's won a couple of Open titles, thinks that in order to be a successful golfer "you've got to have a mean streak in you." Tony Jacklin is yet more relentless: "Life and golf are for the takers. You've got to take it, grab it, and keep it. Never give anything away."

Play happy, or play tough? Be solemn and grim, or casual and carefree? These are hard questions. If you play tough, you can see how Henry Cotton's swing key—"Imagine the ball has little legs, and chop them off"—would come in handy. But then again you may not want to spend your afternoon walking around the course amputating golf balls in your mind. Thoughts of this nature could easily put you into a real funk and spoil your game.

So what's the answer? There is no ultimate answer, of course. "You can never own the secret of golf," said Dave Marr. "You just try to borrow it from time to time." As long as there are golfers, there will be questions probing the mysteries of the game, and as long as there are people with disposable incomes asking those questions, there will be an unending stream of books, videos, and magazine articles seeking to provide answers for them. But as you ponder all this accumulated wisdom, the products of hundreds of years of golf thinking and evolution, always remember the simple words of Mark Calcavecchia, who said: "Golf is just a game—and an idiotic game most of the time."

Curmudgeons

❦

Golf is a good walk spoiled.

—Mark Twain

As hard as it is to believe, there are actually people who do not like golf. There was Twain, and a century later there is Dave Barry: "Nobody knows exactly how golf got started," writes Barry, the self-described "humorist." "Probably what happened was, thousands of years ago, a couple of primitive guys were standing around, holding some odd-shaped sticks, and they noticed a golf ball lying on the grass, and they said, 'Hey! Let's see if we can hit this into a hole!' And then they said, 'Nah. Let's just tell long, boring anecdotes about it instead.' "

Long, boring anecdotes? You're hitting a little too close to home there, Dave. And on a fashion note, he adds that golfers wear "the most unattractive pants money can buy, pants so ugly that they have to be manufactured by blind people in dark rooms." So we don't like your books all that much either, Dave.

But this kind of thing is nothing new. People have been dumping on golfers for as long as there have been golfers. Horace Hutchinson, the British golfer and essayist, describes the nineteenth-century attitude: "It grew common to regard golf as a harmless form of imbecility, holding towards it much the same attitude that the general mind has towards a grown man with a butterfly net and a taste for entomology." Golf was derided as "cow pasture pool." G. K. Chesterton called it "an expensive way of playing marbles." When the game was first catching on in England, in the late 1800s, golf was scorned as an old man's game. One London fishwrap went so far as to say that only stupid people played it, and that stupidity was the most important ingredient for succeeding in it. My, my!

The New York Times was not much better. An 1894 article in the paper of record noted that while the Eastern social elite was picking up on golf, it "seems to find favor with those lovers of outdoor sports who are too stout, too old, or too lazy for any of the severer games" such as tennis or polo. Too stout, too lazy? And they didn't even have golf carts back then.

Much of the anti-golf sentiment of that time had less to do with the game itself and more with the feelings of resentment toward the robber barons who played it. Golf was the plaything of the privileged and the wealthy, and since most ordinary people despised the privileged and wealthy, they despised their game. Mother Jones, the firebrand socialist, was hardly your average Jane on the street, but her sentiments were typical of her day. "Keep up this fight," she told a 1902 rally of striking West Virginia coal miners. "Don't surrender. Pay no attention to the injunction machine at Parkersburg. The federal judge is a scab anyhow. While you starve, he plays golf." Jones was thrown in jail right after making this anti-golf diatribe, and it serves her right.

The perception of golfers as heartless, capitalistic swine persists to this day—"One-gloved beasts in cleats," writes John Updike, "[who] take an open stance on the backs of the poor"—but most of the current knocks on the game come from sportswriters and others who appear to prefer the more macho sports of football and ladies' tag-team wrestling. "Take away the fresh air and 'adorable caddies' and what you have are pro bowlers with suntans," snipes Mike Royko. Is golf a sport? "It can't be a sport if you can play it with a cigarette in your mouth," says another Chicagoan, sportswriter Bill Jauss.

Apparently starved for column ideas, various lazy, overweight, and unathletic sportswriters around the country will, on occasion, attack golf as a game for lazy, overweight, and unathletic people. "The pro links are full of fortyish men in Sansabelt pants and Popsicle shirts riding around in Elmer Fudd cars because walking all that way is too much for them," writes one San Francisco sports columnist. "Which is why golf will always be just a game, not a sport."

Michael Parkinson, one of the wittiest of the contemporary golf curmudgeons, has formed an Anti-Golf Society to stop the spread of "golf blight," as he calls it. He writes, "The scientists and the doom-watchers have got it wrong. The greatest problem facing the world today is not overpopulation or nuclear proliferation, it is golf blight."

He goes on, "Some of us despair for the future of the human race. The golfers are taking over, vast regiments of people whose only justification can be that they provide employment for people who make sad and gaudy trousers" (ah, another fashion critic). He adds that "there is more excitement and spectacle in a competition to decide the world's largest parsnip" than in watching a golf tournament on television, concluding, "Vegetables are more important than golfers, and aesthetically speaking, I'd rather watch a cabbage grow than a man worrying his guts over a two-foot putt."

Vegetables more important than golfers? That's going too far. But parsnips more interesting than TV golf? You know, he may have a point on that one.

Of Time and the Golfer

Golf dispels the myth that older Americans have to be less active or competitive. Ask any middle-aged golfer who's been bested by someone his parents' age. I speak from experience; on the links, youth offers no advantage.

—Vice President Dan Quayle

Golf is derided as a game for old coots, but that's one of its chief virtues. Old coots—uh, seniors—are among the game's most ardent partisans. "Those clubs don't know how old you are," Claudia Trevino told her husband after he turned forty-four and started moaning about how he was getting too "old" for golf. Lee has since learned better. Forty-four is barely out of diapers in golf time. Lots of people twice that age are still playing and enjoying the game.

The tenth earl of Wemyss played well into his nineties, riding a pony around the course. His son, also an avid ball-striker, used to say: "Everybody dies but my father." But his father proved him wrong, finally passing on at ninety-six, and the son became the eleventh earl of Wemyss in his seventies.

Plenty of seniors all over the place have shot their age. "That's no challenge," said one Jimmy Drake, who, at eighty-nine, used to shoot in the 80s. "The challenge is to better it." By and large, though, seniors tend to be less score-oriented than their younger counterparts. Ask a senior if he wants to keep score and he'll probably give you a pained expression and say, "I don't usually keep score. It's too depressing." If he does keep score, he will tend to be a very generous record-keeper, for himself if not for others. As the humorist Abel Kessler has noted, seniors are supposed to have failing memories. But they can remember a bad shot they made on a hole for weeks after.

Some of the most thrilling feats in tournament golf have been turned in by men and women middle-aged or older. Gene Sarazen, age seventy-one, shot two consecutive rounds under 80 at the 1973 British Open at Troon. He missed the cut, but a hole in one at the famous "Postage Stamp" hole helped temper his disappointment. Old Tom Morris won the British Open in 1867. He was forty-six. Ben Hogan, fifty-four, shot a 66 in the third round of the 1967 Masters. Hogan was forty-seven when he nearly won that ever-elusive fifth U.S. Open in 1960. Tied for the lead going into the 17th hole on the final day, he drove into the rough and missed his chance for a tie with the eventual winner, Arnold Palmer. A similar fate befell the fifty-year-old Harry Vardon, who led the 1920 U.S. Open by five strokes with seven holes to go but collapsed under trying wind conditions and lost by a stroke. Hale Irwin won his third Open at age forty-five. Gary Player won the Masters at forty-two, the oldest winner ever until the forty-six-year-old Jack Nicklaus made his heroic charge to win the 1986 Masters. Nicklaus, now past fifty, is not yet finished with regular tournament play, and one suspects he may have a surprise or two left in him, such as his marvelous 63—one stroke off the course record—on the second round at the 1991 Doral Open or his inspired showing at the Masters that spring.

Unquestionably, the greatest older golfer of all time was Sam Snead, who took second at the U.S. Open in 1937 and more than twenty-five years later, won the Greater Greensboro Open, a regular stop on the PGA Tour. At fifty-two years and ten months, Snead was the oldest-ever winner of a regular tour event. Slammin' Sammy won his first PGA title in 1942. In 1974, at 62, he finished third in the PGA, behind only Nicklaus and Trevino. In 1979, then sixty-seven, Snead shot his age in the second round of the Quad Cities Open. He fell off on Saturday, then rebounded with a 66 the next day. This was, remember, a regular PGA event using the championship tees— not one of those shrink-to-fit courses on the present-day seniors circuit.

Of course, Snead took his act onto the Senior Tour, where he continued to thrive. He won thirteen events but at seventy-seven, finally called it quits. "It's a grind trying to beat those sixty-year-old kids out there," he explained.

The reasons for Snead's extraordinary longevity are many. First, his attitude. After so many years of playing the game he could still keep it fresh. "Where Sam excels is in always being able to enjoy the game—in playing it for fun as much as for a living," says an admiring Jack Nicklaus, who has had a few attitude problems himself since entering his sixth decade. Snead's youthful outlook was all the more remarkable considering that until recent years, he had played nearly every week of his life. But he saw his lifelong commitment to the game as a plus, not a negative. "It's like anything else," he said. "You don't lose it as fast if you keep at it. It's when you stop playing and then try to get it back that you've lost it."

Snead played constantly; there was no such thing as a vacation from golf. Why should there be? In Snead's mind, golf *was* a vacation. Another factor that cannot be underestimated were his great physical gifts, notably his suppleness and flexibility. It's common for seniors to lose ten, fifteen, twenty-five yards off their drive, due to the lack of muscle flexibility that comes with increasing age. As a young man the double-jointed Snead used to win bets by touching an eight-foot-high ceiling with his foot while keeping the other foot on the floor; in his seventies, he could still do it.

As he grew older, Snead developed a problem with his putter. This is all too common. Putting requires confidence and steadiness of nerves, qualities that seem to erode over the years. But time, as Snead and so many others will testify, is not the enemy of the golfer as it is in so many other sports. Indeed time can deepen one's appreciation for the game. If you've played golf awhile you have inevitably experienced multiple failures of a humbling nature; these failures consequently enrich your understanding of the difficulties inherent in a well-struck golf shot. Only an older golfer knows true happiness in the game, for he, above all, has an intimate and long-standing acquaintance with the misery it produces.

Ah, but what pleasure awaits those who are willing to suffer for it! John Campbell, a Scottish outdoorsman who lived in the 1800s, was a fisherman and a deer and fox hunter. But his first love was golf. Typically, his putting game betrayed him more and more the older he got, and he could not buy a putt until one day, toward the end of his life, he sunk a long, twisting thirty-five-footer across a hard green. "What a splendid putt!" he cried. "In my time I have had the best grouse shooting in Scotland, and the best river fishing and the best deer stalking, and I have kept the best [fox] hunters at Melton; but I am thankful to say I can now dream about a putt!"

The King of Golf Comedy

❦

I'd give up golf if I didn't have so many sweaters.

—Bob Hope

Henny Youngman has his violin; George Burns has a cigar; Bing had his pipe. For Bob Hope, it's a golf club. Hope once demonstrated his swing to Pat Bradley, the tour pro. "What do I do next?" Hope asked her. "Wait till the pain dies down," she replied. Another time Hope was in a foursome with Jack Nicklaus, who launched a long drive down the center of the fairway. "How come I can't drive like that?" Hope asked. "You'd get more distance if you took the head covers off your woods," Nicklaus said dryly.

Hope has a million golf stories. Some of them are even true. Playing in a pro-am with Jan Stephenson, he asked, "How do you like my game?" Stephenson responded, "It's all right, but I still prefer golf." Hope's real game is making people laugh, and the secret of his golf humor may be that he's not afraid to make himself the butt of his jokes. "Golf's a hard game to figure," he wrote. "One day you'll go out and slice it and shank it, hit into all the traps and miss every green. The next day you go out and for no reason at all you really stink." Chatting with onetime PGA champion Bob Tway, Hope said admiringly, "You go into those bunkers with such confidence. When I go in, I bring along two days of provisions and a change of linen." After another round, he said, "I'm playing pretty well today. I only fell out of the cart twice. Titleist has offered me a big contract not to play its ball."

Hope was never a great golfer, but he was not as bad as he lets on. In the early 1950s, when Hope was forty-eight, he got down to a four handicap before the British Amateur. Not many comics can claim that. Like his buddy Bing Crosby, Hope started playing golf while working in vaudeville and radio in New York City in the 1920s. Hope lived on Central Park West and played all the courses in the area. By the late 1930s Hollywood was calling, and he joined Crosby at the glamorous Lakeside Golf Club in Los Angeles. Hope once hit a hole in one at Lakeside with Fred Astaire in his foursome.

A photograph of Bobby Jones, his golfing idol, hung in his dressing room at Paramount Pictures. Though pool was his game when he was young, Hope took to golf with the zeal of the newly converted. It was only natural that many of his playing partners came from the movie community. As Hope drank one night in London with Humphrey Bogart, who was himself a low handicapper, Bogey wondered what it would be like to tee one off Hope's famous ski nose. Hope supposedly lay down on the floor of their hotel and put some gum on his nose, which Bogart used as a tee.

Hope and Crosby, who made seven "road" pictures together, were the most popular comedy team in America, and they often took their act onto the golf course. "They're making a movie of Bing's round yesterday," said Hope. "It stars Bela Lugosi." Touché, Bob, now over to Bing: "You want to know about Bob Hope's swing? I've seen better swings on a condemned playground." To raise money for the war effort the twosome journeyed around the country on the Victory Caravan, attracting huge crowds wherever they went. "One day twenty-eight thousand people showed up to watch us in Chicago," Hope told Dwayne Netland. "I don't think many of them had been on a golf course before. They'd come to a ball in the fairway and stand around in a circle. We'd have to say, 'Open up, please. We go *that* way.'" Before the war, Crosby invited some of his friends (including Hope) down to Rancho Santa Fe to play a little golf and drink a few drinks with the touring pros. After the war, in 1947, the Crosby Pro-Am moved up to the Monterey Peninsula. Later Hope got his own tournament and a spot on the tour, choosing the hot and dry climes of Palm Desert in contrast to the wet and sloppy coastal weather of brother Bing's.

Hope has played golf with kings, presidents, generals, prime ministers, movie stars, congressmen, industrial tycoons—and made jokes about everybody and everything. On Clint Eastwood: "He's easy to spot on a golf course. He's the only guy who carries his putter in a holster." On golf on the rainy Monterey Peninsula: "I've often wondered what it was like to play inside a ball washer." On snooty Cypress Point: "They had a very successful membership drive last month. They drove out forty members." On the current Senior Tour: "I didn't realize how long some of these fellows had been around until I saw a guy yesterday signing his scorecard with a quill." On Arnold Palmer: "Arnie's not in a real good humor today. He just saw a TV commercial that he wasn't in." Hope was playing with Irv Kupcinet, the Chicago newspaper columnist, and noted that Kup had four-putted the last green. "I know," said Kupcinet. "I like to putt."

On one of his many tours to entertain American troops overseas, Hope stayed overnight on an aircraft carrier, the USS *Ticonderoga*. The morning after the show the ship's captain surprised him with a gift of a bag of golf balls. In the vicinity was another battleship, which pulled alongside the *Ticonderoga*. Hope, then, had the singular challenge of seeing if he could drive a golf ball two hundred yards across the open seas to the deck of the waiting ship. Hope may have been thinking of moments such as this one when he said, "They ask me when I'm going to retire. Retire? Play golf, tell a few jokes, and have so many friends all over the world? My whole career has been a round of golf."

Golf Humor

❧

A frustrated hacker hits a ball onto an ant hill. He swings and misses, and swings and misses, until he has completely destroyed the ant hill. But the ball is untouched—a fact that does not go unnoticed by the two remaining ants in the area. "If we're going to live, we better get on the ball," says one ant to the other. "It's the only safe place."

Every golfer must be able to tell at least one golf joke. It's in the rules. It's also a well-known fact that certain country clubs will not let you in their front door until you've told a joke.

A novice golfer has just taken a big divot with his shot. "What do I do with this?" he asks his caddie as he holds up the piece of turf. "Take it home," replies the caddie, "and practice on it."

If you're not a natural-born storyteller and the thought of telling a joke to a group of men in polyester pants strikes terror in your heart, do not despair. A golf joke is, by definition, corny. The joke itself is not as important as the fact that you are telling it, sharing it with your golf brethren in the age-old tradition of comitatus. Even the worst golf jokes will receive a grudging acknowledgment.

Two golfers are standing on the green. One lies eight, the other lies nine. The fellow who lies nine picks up his ball. "It's your hole," he says. "My short game is lousy."

It's a given that a golf joke never reads as well in print as it sounds when someone tells it. It's all delivery and timing, says Bob Hope, who has told more golf jokes than any nine people alive. Also, knowing your audience is important. But Hope says that over the years he has noticed that more and more people understand his golf references—an unofficial indication, yet one not lightly to be dismissed, of the continuing popularity of the game.

A priest with a bad hook is about to tee off, but he faces a looming water hazard on his left, and he's not sure if he should play a new ball or an old one. "God, please give me directions," he says, eyes skyward. Suddenly, a burst of thunder and lightning and from out of the clouds comes a voice: "Play the new ball!"

So the priest breaks a new ball out of the package and he's about to hit when there's another crackle of thunder: "Take a practice swing," says the voice from above. Obediently, the priest takes a practice swing, followed by one more peal of thunder from God. "Better play the old ball," He says.

The diety figures often in golf jokes. So do wives. Do women on the golf course tell husband jokes? And are they as bad as most wife jokes?

A man is trying to convince his friend Harold to join him in a foursome that afternoon. "I'd love to," Harold says, "but I promised my wife I'd spend some time with her and the kids." "Aw, come on," says the golfer. "Forget about your wife. Are you a man or a mouse?" "I'm a man," says Harold. "My wife's afraid of a mouse."

"No sport," says Rick Reilly, "lends itself to humor like golf, probably for the same reason there are so many earthquake jokes." What distinguishes golf, too, is that the target of much of its humor are golfers themselves. The quickest way to a golfer's funny bone is by spoofing him and his magnificent obsession, the folly of which he knows so well.

A frustrated golfer has just slashed his wrists and he's bleeding to death as his friend walks in on him. "What are you doing?" cries the friend. "You've cut your wrists!"

"I hate this lousy game," says the frustrated golfer. "I hate it so much. I don't want to go on living and I never want to play again."

"Oh, that's too bad," says the friend. "I came over to see if you wanted to play tomorrow."

"Oh, really," says the bleeding golfer. "What time?"

Lightning

The number one rule concerning lightning on a golf course is: Don't get hit by it. Lee Trevino had a foolproof way to avoid being hit: "Hold your one-iron over your head. Not even God can hit a one-iron." But apparently Trevino didn't get that one-iron up quickly enough because he was hit by a bolt from the sky during a tournament. Afterward his wife called him to see if he was okay. "I feel great," said Trevino. "For the first time in my life I was six foot two." Even so, it would be prudent for golfers to treat lightning much as Bob Hope does. "Personally, if I'm on a golf course and lightning starts, I get indoors fast," says Hope. "If God wants to play through, I let him."

Trees

Joyce Kilmer may have been wild about trees, but golfers have their doubts. A few golfers resort to Kilmer's game—poetry—to describe their love-hate relationship with those tall, leafy things:

> *I know only God can make a tree*
> *But on the golf course they sure bug me.*
> *I hate those trees whose leafy arms extend*
> *To snag a perfect 4-iron that I send.*

I love their beauty—don't get me wrong.
But let's keep 'em in the forest
Where they belong.

This was written by Bill Sinai, a retired California dentist, but the sentiment is shared by anyone who has ever wielded a MacGregor or a Yonex with gravity of purpose. Trees are lovely to look at, and sometimes the ricochet effect can work to your advantage. But let's face it. Mostly the damn things just get in the way.

A while ago at the Olympic Club in San Francisco they cut back some branches of a tree on the 8th hole, and more than one hundred balls fell out. That's one hundred perfectly good golf shots foiled by one lousy tree. They should've leveled the sucker.

There are almost as many tree stories in golf as there are caddie stories. One of the best is about the Glasgow, Scotland golfer whose tee shot hit a beech tree. The tree groaned, cracked, and with a mighty thud, keeled over. Ah, sweet revenge!

Arnold Palmer, like all golfers, had more than his share of run-ins with trees. In one tournament he hit three straight shots into the limb of a tree, each time the ball caroming out-of-bounds. Palmer, furious, carded an eight on the hole, but he—or one of his supporters—got the last laugh. The next morning the obstructing branch had been removed, and as one spectator noted, "it didn't look like it had been sawed off."

Arnie had another brush with a tree at the Crosby Pro-Am, back in the days when he was still contending for titles. In the thick of the hunt on the last day, his second shot on the 14th at Pebble grazed the branches of a cypress and rabbit-hopped into the red zone. His concentration blown, Palmer took a nine on the hole and fell out of contention. That same evening a ferocious storm rolled in from the Pacific, uprooting the tree and blowing it to the ground. Too late to help Palmer, but at least a rough sort of golf justice was achieved.

When Johnny Miller was a kid, his dad used to take him into a grove of trees, drop a bag of balls on the ground, and say, "Hit through the openings." But that didn't help Miller at the 1982 Memorial at Muirfield Village, when he hit the same tree three times on the same hole. Trailing by one stroke with one hole to go, Miller, in a bunker, had to clear a pine tree to reach the green. His first ball hit the tree, about twenty feet away, and bounced back to him. His next ball hit the tree again, but at least he cleared the trap. Thinking it was impossible to hit the tree a third time, he aimed for the green once more and achieved the impossible. Miller lost the tournament and the pine barely registered a scratch.

Trees have factored into golf history in other ways as well. During the 1970s, in a period of widespread drug experimentation in America, some of the PGA's finest were questioned about their possible use of marijuana or other illicit substances. Doug Sanders dismissed this as nonsense. "At golf," he said, "you have to be mentally alert. You can't lean against a tree that isn't there."

The most famous tree of recent golf times is the Hinkle Tree. At the 1979 U.S. Open in Inverness, Lon Hinkle saw something that no one else did on the par-5 8th. To the left of the teeing area was an opening between the trees. A light bulb clicked on in Hinkle's mind, and he drove down the adjoining fairway for a birdie that was as easy as it was fast and loose. Aghast at Hinkle's slyness and its potential repercussions, USGA officials hastily purchased a twenty-five-foot spruce tree and at sunrise the next morning, planted it in the opening, thus blocking any further Hinkle-type maneuvers.

A former USGA president, describing how a golf course changes over the years, writes, "One problem [that] trees frequently develop is that they get bigger and their branches spread." Yes, that's a problem all right, one that was forgotten by a young golfer playing a round with wily old Sam Snead. Standing at the tee, the young buck couldn't decide whether or not to try to drive over a stand of tall trees on one side of the fairway.

"Son," said Snead, then in his sixties, "when I was your age I could clear those trees easy."

Faced with a clear challenge, the youngster lined it up and drove his ball smack-dab into the trees.

"Of course," said Snead after the young man had hit, "when I was your age, those trees were only twenty feet tall."

Quiet, Please

Golf has in common with funerals and tennis the need for quiet. This is due to the presence of men like Greg Norman, who once glared at an earthworm as he was about to hit, and Sam Snead, who, writes Patrick Campbell, was known to "threaten legal action against people dropping pins half a mile away while he was trying to hole a four-foot putt."

Messrs. Snead and Norman are no different from any of us. We all need to be protected from earthworms and falling pins. "The least thing upset him on the links," P. G. Wodehouse wrote of a golfer. "He missed short putts because of the uproar of butterflies in the adjoining meadow." And oh yes, the butterflies! What a racket they cause!

Golf galleries know the paramount importance of quietude and accordingly maintain a vow of silence. "I like golf because when somebody tells the gallery to be quiet, they get quiet," says Mark McGwire, the Oakland A's first baseman. "Try that in baseball and they get louder."

Some golf spectators are more cooperative than others, though.

Stranded in a bunker and preparing to hit out, Arnold Palmer heard a boy talking in the crowd around him. Arnold stepped back, and the boy's mother quickly told him to hush. The boy started crying. After a minute there was quiet again, but Palmer had to step away once more because there was no mistaking the muffled sounds of the boy choking. The boy's mother had her hand over his mouth and he couldn't breathe.

"Hey," Palmer said to the mom, "it's okay. Don't choke him. This isn't that important."

Some golfers might have let the kid twist awhile longer, at least until they got their shot off, but the beneficent Palmer knew better. In golf, one must confront the hard reality that no matter how quiet it is, one might still botch the shot. There is the case of Scott Verplank at a recent PGA championships. A baby in the gallery was crying, and Verplank could not attempt his putt. "Quit crying," somebody called out, "he hasn't missed it yet." The baby finally quieted down, Verplank went forward—and blew the putt.

School of Hard Knocks

Michael Parkinson, president of the Anti-Golf Society, cannot fathom why anyone would want to spectate at a golf match. "One of life's great mysteries is just what do golfers think they are playing at," he writes. "But even more mysterious is what those spectators who traipse around golf courses are looking for."

Galleries, in point of fact, serve many useful purposes. Their presence has influenced many a tournament outcome. Golfers listen for the reaction of galleries on the course; if they hear a cheer go up, meaning that their rival has sunk a birdie putt, it sometimes influences them to rush their next shot or change their strategy on a hole. Additionally, galleries help the pros by stopping their balls. Lee Trevino has seen a ball land in a cup of beer and a man's pants pocket; one mischievous ball even found its way into a woman's brassiere. Other spectators have had the misfortune of stopping balls with their heads.

One thinks of the crowd-scattering drives of Gerald Ford in this connection, but the best story of this type involves Tommy Bolt, who accidentally hit a man with a tee ball during an exhibition some time ago in Pittsburgh. It was a par 3, and Bolt hit a screamer into the crowd gathered around the edges of the green. People yelled "Fore!" but to no avail: the ball conked a man right in his forehead, the ball hopping crazily onto the green as the man fell to the deck in a heap. Bolt and everyone else rushed to give aid to the man, who was told to lie still and not move while a doctor was called. It looked serious.

Since Bolt couldn't really do anything more to help, he decided to go ahead and play out the hole. "Anybody see where my ball went?" he asked.

"Yeah, Tommy," said a helpful spectator, "it bounced onto the green over there."

At long last the doctor arrived and he bent over the man on the ground. His vital signs seemed fine, but his eyes were glazed over and he seemed only dimly aware of his surroundings. "Can you talk?" the doctor asked.

"Yeah, sure," said the man. "Did Bolt make the putt?"

The Moose, the Walrus, Wonder Woman, and Deadman Jack

In professional golf, as in other sports, part of the fun is in the nicknames. Curtis Strange is the Piranha because, as Lee Trevino says, "if he gets a chance, he'll eat you up." Trevino himself is the Merry Mex or Super Mex, and his gallery followers in the late sixties and seventies were known as Lee's Fleas, a takeoff on the masses of enlistees in Arnie's Army. Palmer, the commander of this legion, was the General to his troops, but among his peers his muscular physique and attacking style earned him the sobriquet the Bull. People were less kind to Nicklaus in those days. The chubby wunderkind was Ohio Fats or the Fat Man, as well as the more complimentary Golden Bear.

Speaking of bears, Mike Souchak, who once shot a 60 in a PGA tournament, was known as Smokey the Bear for his resemblance to the old fire-prevention symbol. Then there is the soft-spoken Ben Crenshaw, aka Gentle Ben. While we're touring about the animal kingdom, we might want to get out of our cars and see the Moose, Julius Boros. Boros trudged slowly and ponderously to get to his next shot, hence the title. This is in contrast to Light Horse Harry Cooper, who played golf at a gallop. Circling overhead majestically is the Hawk—Ben Hogan, of course. Hogan was also the Iceman, and there never was a more fitting nickname than that. Gardner Dickinson, a member of the generation of golfers after Hogan, wore a white cap like Hogan and copied the great man's deliberate style. But Gardner was not Hogan's match as a golfer—who was?—and his contemporaries rather cruelly referred to him as Chicken Hawk.

Nicknames do not necessarily flatter. Pat "Lay Up" Bradley was

called that early in her career because of a tendency to take the easy way out. Over the years she became bolder with her shots and the appellation fell away.

"Concentration Henry" sounds like a smooth-talking, dice-rolling character in a Damon Runyon story. In fact his last name was Cotton and he was a very determined, very gifted English golfer from a half century ago. It was Walter Hagen—the Haig, Sir Walter— who gave Cotton his nickname. A contemporary of Hagen's was the Squire, what they called Gene Sarazen for his country-gentleman tastes.

Another thirties-era golfer was the diminutive Paul Runyan, or Little Poison, a nickname shared by the Hall of Fame ballplayer Lloyd Waner. If the game is baseball, the Babe is Ruth; if it's golf, it's Zaharias. The golfing Babe used to wow galleries with the length of her drives; so does the LPGA pro Laura Davies. Some have called Davies the new Big Momma, in deference to the original Big Momma, Joanne Carner, who was also known as the Great Gundy before her marriage. (Her maiden name was Gunderson.) In 1978, after Nancy Lopez won five tournaments in a row in her rookie season, the press dubbed her Wonder Woman. Judy Rankin agreed: "They've got the wrong Wonder Woman on TV," she said in awe of Nancy's smashing debut.

Some years ago Craig "the Walrus" Stadler was the center of a controversy in which he knelt on a towel to hit a shot from under a tree. Ignorant of the rule that prohibits building a stance, Stadler did not penalize himself for this transgression and was disqualified from the tournament. Many people thought this was unnecessarily harsh, and they described the official who penalized Stadler as the Marquis de Sod.

"The Apple Tree Gang" sounds like the title of a Disney movie, but it was actually the name for those hardy golf pioneers who founded the St. Andrew's Golf Club in New York, the oldest-running club in the States. After moving their headquarters around a bit they settled on a course distinguished by the great number of apple trees on it. The influence of the St. Andrew's club was so great on turn-of-the-century golf that a local judge, inspecting a new course being built at Shinnecock Hills on Long Island, remarked that Shinnecock couldn't possibly be an authentic golf course because it didn't have any apple trees on it.

Great golfers can come in twos, threes, and fours. "The Great Triumvirate" was Harry Vardon, John Henry Taylor, and James Braid, the best golfers in the world circa 1900. The U.S. version of the Triumvirate was Ben Hogan, Slammin' Sammy Snead, and Byron Nelson. Nobody ever had a better year than Nelson in 1945; he won everything in sight, including eleven consecutive tournaments. (Along with Harold "Jug" McSpaden, Nelson was also one of the Gold Dust Twins, so named because medical deferments kept them out of World War II and enabled them to stay home and play golf.) Citing frazzled nerves, the sweet-swinging Nelson retired in 1949, leaving Snead and Hogan without a third leg in their triad. But in the 1960s a new trio of weighty historical significance came along: the "Big Three" of Palmer, Nicklaus, and Player. Not to slight the women, they had a

"Big Four" in the fifties: Patty Berg, Louise Suggs, Betty Jameson, and Babe Zaharias.

Another name for Byron Nelson was the Mechanical Man, which is akin to what they called Gene "the Machine" Littler, who hit fairways with machinelike regularity. Similarly, Mike Reid is Radar for the accuracy of his tee balls. But "Fuzzy" Zoeller's nickname does not refer to his golf game or the hair on his face or anything you might think. His full name is Frank Urban Zoeller, and F.U.Z. evolved into Fuzzy.

Al Geiberger was Skippy, due to the peanut butter sandwiches he ate on the course to give him energy. Billy Casper's strict diet favored buffalo and reindeer steaks—hence, Buffalo Bill. Tony Lema had more sophisticated tastes; after his first victory on the tour he treated the press to glasses of the bubbly, beginning a custom that he followed after every tournament win, including the 1964 British Open. Because of this, and because he died too young, Champagne Tony Lema shall always be fondly remembered.

Mason Rudolph was the Spy, while Miller Barber was Mr. X, so dubbed for his enigmatic look behind dark sunglasses. There was Walter Travis, a terrific 1900s-era golfer who took up golf in his midthirties and thus was known as the Old Man. If this makes you feel old, at least you're not dead—as in "Deadman" Jack McGowan, a former touring pro. Deadman Jack got his name from a habit he had of calling out after every bad shot he hit, "I'm dead, I'm dead! Oh, man, I'm just dead over there!" He's dead, and we're outta here.

The Yips

The yips are not funny. The yips are painful, especially to the golfer who has them. "For me they started with a feeling of tension in my stomach," said Sam Snead. "It would tie up into a knot. Then the tension would start spreading all over, into my chest, down my arms, and finally, to the tips of my fingers." Gordon Jones, a Senior Tour golfer, is more succinct: "It's like holding a rattlesnake, and you don't know which end is the head." Older golfers tend to get the yips the most, but they can strike anybody at any time. In the words of Henry Longhurst, "Once you've had 'em, you've got 'em."

Tommy Armour is said to have coined the term—"that ghastly time when, with the first movement of the putter, the golfer blacks out, loses sight of the ball, and hasn't the remotest idea of what to do with the putter or occasionally, that he is holding a putter at all." The yips are known by a variety of names: the shakes, whiskey fingers, the jumps. The British refer to them as the twitches or the twitch. A recent UCLA neurological study defined them as "a motor phenomenon that affects golfers and consists of involuntary movements in the course of execution of focused, finely controlled, skilled motor behavior." Plain and simple, it's the heebie-jeebies.

The yips are intimately caught up in the mysteries of putting, but to miss a putt is not necessarily to yip. Nor can the yips be defined simply as a bad putt, or a string of bad putts. The yips are something different, and worse. They attack the skilled and the unskilled, those who are playing for money and those who are not, but they are most dramatic when they show up in big-time tournament play. On the first hole of sudden death at the 1989 Masters, Scott Hoch, a run-of-the-mill tour veteran, was two and a half feet away from immortality and his first major. He stepped up to the putt—and backed off.

"That's the worst thing you can do," he said later. "Step up to a golf shot without a clear idea in your head." Hesitation breeds doubt, and the yips feed on doubt. Hoch stepped up again and ran his two-and-a-half footer five feet past the hole. On the next hole Nick Faldo buried a twenty-five-footer that buried Hoch as well.

It probably wouldn't make Hoch feel any better to know that much the same thing happened to Hubert Green a decade earlier at Augusta. Three strokes up at the close of the third round, Green crashed and burned on the final day but still had a chance to force a playoff if he could nail a three-footer on 18. He missed it. After play was concluded on Sunday, after the spectators had all gone home, after the green coat had been handed out and all the television cameras turned off, Hubie went back out to try that putt again.

And again. And again. And again.

"I had to find out if I misread it or mishit it," he told a reporter. And?

"I read it right. When the pressure was on, I just didn't hit it straight."

Ah, but those three-footers are killers, aren't they? "Putting affects the nerves more than anything," said Byron Nelson, who quit the professional tour at thirty-four because of the strain it put on his nerves. "I would actually get nauseated over three-footers during my prime. Missing a short putt is about the most humiliating thing in the world because you're supposed to make it." Nelson had the yips so bad once that he hit a four-foot putt forty feet past the hole. That's not as crazy as it sounds. Bobby Jones saw Wild Bill Mehlhorn twitch on impact and send a three-foot putt zooming past the hole across the green into a bunker on the far side.

The yips span the generations. They are one of golf's dreaded universals, along with quadruple bogeys and whiffing on your tee ball. Francis Ouimet, in his historic 1913 U.S. Open win, got a bad case of the yips even as he stood on the 72nd green with the championship safely in hand. "For the first time [in the tournament] I thought about the championship, and it was almost too much," he said, describing his feelings at the time. "Suddenly I couldn't breathe. The green began heaving beneath me. I could not see the hole." Harry Vardon, one of the players whom Ouimet was thrashing in that Open, would have empathized with what young Francis was going through at that moment, for he had experienced similar sensations. The Englishman could even anticipate when they were coming on. "As I stood addressing the ball, I would watch for my right hand to jump," he wrote. "At the end of two seconds I would not be looking at the ball at all. My gaze would become riveted on my right hand. . . . Directly, as I felt that it was about to jump, I would snatch at the ball in a desperate effort to play the shot before the involuntary movement would take effect. Up would go my head and body with a start, and off would go the ball, anywhere but the proper line."

The great Ben Hogan was a sufferer, too. Yipes, he had the yips! On the final round of the 1954 Masters he three-putted 13, missed a four-footer on 15, and three-putted 17. Still, with all that, he had a chance to win on 18 if he could reel in a six-footer. Stepping off the green, Hogan must have taken one hundred practice strokes, trying different grips, hand positions, follow-throughs. Do we need to say it? He missed.

After another breakout of the yips at a U.S. Open, Hogan received thousands of letters of advice from people offering their homemade remedies. But sad to say, there may be no permanent cure for the yips except, perhaps, for a change in attitude. After all, as Fuzzy Zoeller says, "there's nothing wrong with four-putting. It just means you missed the third one."

Gassing

❦

Gassing is not yipping, but it's close. Gassing is leak city, going to the apple orchard, gagging, gorking—in short, choking. To choke is not necessarily to yip, but both are to be avoided in any case.

Just ask Patty Sheehan. After her Los Altos home fell down in the devastating 1989 San Francisco Bay Area earthquake, the whole world fell on top of her at the U.S. Women's Open the next year. Sheehan, one of the best women players in the world, rebounded from the earthquake to post three wins on the LPGA Tour. But what she wanted most was the Open, an event she had failed to win while finishing second three times. More determined than ever, she got out of the chute fast in 1990, piling up a seemingly insurmountable nine-stroke margin by the middle of the third round. She was playing splendidly, just cruising along, and a new Women's Open record for lowest number of total strokes appeared likely.

Then the wheels came off, the engine blew, and Sheehan was ejected into the worst sort of golfer ignominy.

She gave up five strokes of her nine-shot lead on the back nine of the third round, then gave away the other four on the front nine of round four. Because of bad weather in Duluth, Georgia, where the Open was held, the final thirty-six holes were all played on Sunday. It was the worst day of Sheehan's golfing life. Nothing went right, and it brought back bitter memories of the year before when she couldn't recover from a double bogey late in the final round and lost to Betsy King. The steady-as-she-goes King beat her again in 1990, taking her second straight Open, and after Sheehan broke down in tears in front of the television cameras following her collapse, Betsy tried to console her.

"It happens," she said. "Lots of times you win events and you don't play well. They're not going to know what happened [to Patty] down the road. They're just going to see the winner's name and not know what occurred."

Unfortunately, that's not always the way it works. Sheehan's collapse was the big story of that Open, and they're going to tell it for as long as people tell stories about all the bad things that can happen to you when you play golf.

A quick quiz. When you mention the 1966 men's U.S. Open, do you first think of Billy Casper, the ultimate winner, or do you think of Arnold Palmer's act of self-immolation on the back nine that final day? Case closed.

No matter how many Pennzoil or Hertz commercials he does, Palmer will never be able to live down the fact that he blew a seven-stroke lead with nine holes to go in that Open. Seven strokes, nine holes—and he coughed it up. So completely did Palmer fall apart that if Casper had made a fourteen-foot birdie putt on 18, he would've won outright and not had to go to the trouble of finishing off the humiliated Palmer in a playoff the next day.

One of the common characteristics in the Palmer and Sheehan debacles is that both were challenging records at the time of their collapses. A birdie on 15 in the second round put Sheehan at ten under par—the earliest that any golfer, man or woman, had reached such a mark in an Open. "It seemed she might set a record that would last forever," said one observer. Similarly, at the beginning of that fateful final nine, Palmer was less concerned with Casper than with the ghost of Ben Hogan. He had a real shot at Hogan's Open record of 276 (since eclipsed by Nicklaus) and quite consciously, set his sights on breaking it.

Palmer himself concedes that he may have been guilty of that old Greek thing known as hubris—the sin of excessive pride, or counting your birdies before they hatch. Hubris may be one reason why golfers go into the tank. Another is the undeniable, bone-rattling fact of pressure. Dave Marr gave as good a description as there is of what it feels like to play the final holes of a big tournament, with everything on the line and the whole world watching: "It's like walking into a certain room in a big dark house when you were a kid—you get this fear that haunts you." Boo!

And the pressure just builds and builds. Unlike other professional sports, where the playing fields are constant and uniform, a golfer must face a constantly changing terrain. And he must do this by himself without benefit of teammates to shield his mistakes. When he screws up, it's there for all to see. Each new hole, in turn, presents a different picture than the last and provides new obstacles to be overcome, fresh reasons for worry. Golfers are big worriers. And at a course such as Augusta National or one of the British Open sites, where the ghosts of golfers and their past humiliations loom around every corner, there is indeed much cause for worry. A golfer may dread a certain hole or set of holes, such as the Amen Corner at Augusta, knowing in the pit of his stomach that it looms up ahead and there is no avoiding it. And then he begins to look ahead too much, and he loses his concentration, and suddenly, it's gone.

Henry Longhurst writes, "There can hardly be a golfer who has not in his humble way had the mortification of seeing a winning lead crumble away a stroke or two at first, then the gathering momentum, the avalanche, and the dread realization that he is doomed." Be they humble or proud, all golfers, in the end, are doomed, and there's a little bit of Patty Sheehan in us all.

A Tale of Two Phenoms: Robert and Bobby

The future would appear to be bright for Robert "Don't-call-me-Bob" Gamez, the richly talented young man who dropped out of college to pursue fame and fortune on the PGA Tour and promptly achieved both with a win in his first-ever tournament, the 1990 Tucson Open. Then only twenty-one, Gamez followed this stunning success with more stunning successes, notably his dramatic victory over Greg Norman at Bay Hill the same year. In that event the Las Vegas–ite hit the jackpot with an improbable 176-yard pitch for an eagle two on the final hole of the tournament, giving the hard-luck Australian another second place to add to his résumé. After Gamez's seeing-eye 7-iron cleared some water and skipped across the green into the hole, fellow pro Paul Azinger exulted: "The kid doesn't know that he's supposed to be afraid!" "What's there to be afraid of?" said Gamez when told of Azinger's remark. "It was the exact shot I pictured myself hitting."

The clear-sighted Gamez would seem to possess the bravura personality needed to withstand the pressures of life on the PGA Tour. But nothing is certain, and confidence alone won't get you there.

Bobby Clampett was another confident young man who seemed to have the golfing world by the tail. He was a can't-miss. Make a bust of him and ship it straight to Pinehurst. The kid was a lock, ten or twelve majors easy—the next Nicklaus. Like Gamez, he was a College Player of the Year with All-American credentials. He grew up playing in the golf wonderland of Carmel Valley and the Monterey Peninsula, and like Gamez, he was chock-full of postadolescent bluster. Clampett once compared himself to Nicklaus, but unlike Jack, Bobby could see no flaws in his own game. At the 1979 U.S. Open, while still an amateur (Clampett won several prestigious amateur titles), Bobby missed the cut. But USGA officials asked him to play with another golfer as a nonscoring partner. Clampett obliged and began hitting tee shots from his knees to entertain the fans. The men in blue coats tossed him out on his curly locks, but so what? Mozart had behavior problems too, right? There would be plenty of other opportunities for the boy genius.

Clampett's mechanical swing drew criticism, but in 1982, all the gears were clicking in unison at the British Open. Barely old enough to take a legal drink, in only his second year as a professional, Clampett appeared on the verge of a major breakthrough, shooting a 67 in the first round at Royal Troon followed by a 66 the next day. After two rounds the kid was eleven under par and leading by five strokes. After back-to-back birdies on 4 and 5 Saturday, Clampett was up by seven strokes on a field that included Tom Watson, Nicklaus, and Lee Trevino. Seven strokes! He was not only winning the tournament, he was running away with it.

There is a sad inevitability to what happened next. Up by so many early in the day, he barely made it out of the third round alive. Right after his two birdies, Clampett hit his tee ball on 6 into a bunker. Then his recovery got him into more trouble in another bunker. Then came another bunker. After taking an eight on the hole he staggered to a 78 for the round, though he should probably have been thankful. It could have been worse.

The next day, it got worse. He bogeyed 5, 7, 8, and 9, free-falling out of contention into a tie for tenth place overall, a respectable showing under normal circumstances but a shattering disappointment considering what might have been. "What might have been" is a good summation of the Clampett career, although he continues to knock about the circuit hopeful of rediscovering that boyhood magic. For whatever reason, he never fulfilled his early promise and never again came as close to winning a major as he did at Royal Troon.

"Golf, like art, is a goddess whom we woo in early youth if we would win her," said H. Rider Haggard. And sometimes, even if she is wooed assiduously, that fickle goddess will rise up and *crush* you. Watch out, Robert Gamez.

Baby Golf

❦

Speaking of phenoms, how about Phil Mickelson? He won the Tucson Open, too, the year after Robert Gamez, only Phil was still an amateur when he did it. Phil, a lefty, is another with his sights set on the big time. People are comparing him to a young Nicklaus, and not even Big Jack won a PGA event while still an amateur. In addition, Phil has won two NCAA titles and the U.S. Amateur, played in the Walker

Cup, been on the cover of *Golf Digest*, and teed off with Nick Faldo in the first round of the Masters *and* shot a 69. It is hoped that young Phil is taking accounting courses at Arizona State to keep track of all the money he's going to make once he gets out.

Though only in his early twenties, Phil has already been playing golf for two decades. He started when he was still in diapers, at age one and a half, learning to hit balls in a practice area set up by his parents in the backyard of their San Diego home. Mickelson says he's fascinated by the legend of Bobby Jones, who was a baby phenom himself, and that the reason he stayed in college rather than go for instant pro riches was to make his mark in amateur golf history the same as Jones did.

An even more remarkable golfing prodigy may be Eldrick "Tiger" Woods, who, according to legend, shot a 48 on the back nine of the Navy Golf Course in Cypress, California, when he was three. Among other things, this feat—challenged by many, it is true—earned him a guest spot on "The Mike Douglas Show," where he dueled Bob Hope in a putting contest. At age five, Tiger, by then a seasoned media pro, appeared on "That's Incredible!"

Tiger is a teenager now, and he continues to amaze. He has been known to hit drives in competition well over 300 yards, and by the age of thirteen he had already sunk five holes in one, enough to last an average lifetime. At fifteen, he just missed qualifying for the 1991 Los Angeles Open and becoming the youngest person ever to compete in a PGA Tour event. "The game has never never seemed hard," says Tiger. "I don't know why, but I've always been good."

We're happy to hear that, Tiger, but you'd better not rest on your laurels because there's plenty of competition out there just drooling to take your place. All across America legions of little chubby-legged tykes, wrapped in Huggies and wielding cut-down clubs, are being introduced to the game by their well-meaning, if perhaps a tad pushy, parents. One of the most noteworthy of these baby golfers is Brent Paladino, age five. A resident of Connecticut, Brent is said to hit three hundred balls a day, calling out "Fade" or "Draw" depending on where he plans for his shot to go.

Brent began playing when he was one and a half, which, judging by the examples of Tiger and Phil, may be just about right for the cultivation of a golfing prodigy. Brent has demonstrated his golfing talents on "Late Night With David Letterman" and exhibited an obsessiveness about the game that may well evoke the admiration of more senior golf nuts. Once, in the middle of a dream, he called out in his sleep, "I'm stuck in a sand trap!" He scribbles drawings of golf holes on restaurant napkins and would rather watch a Curtis Strange video than Teenage Mutant Ninja Turtles. In the dead of winter, with his father watching from the car with the heater running, little Brent can be found out on the putting green practicing his stroke. He's a lock within 10 feet, says Dad.

To Brent Paladino and all the other infant up-and-comers, we can only offer our hearty encouragement. It's a great game, and if you can avoid early burnout, you should look forward to a lifetime of good times, if not necessarily PGA riches, on the golf course. But there is one danger lurking out there that you may not be aware of. Some of your frustrated, bogey-making elders can be pretty ornery at times, and they may not take kindly to the sight of a pipsqueak, runny-nosed pre-schooler chipping out of the sand and then knocking down a 10-foot putt. They may, in fact, want to wring your cute and chubby neck. So, be respectful of your elders. At the very least, wait until you're out of diapers before you start showing them up.

The Wide, Wide World of Golf

◦◦◦

A hundred years ago, virtually no one played golf outside Great Britain—and even at that, only select circles of people within Britain. The United States was just being introduced to the game. Now, nearing the end of the century, over 20 million Americans play golf with an estimated 1 million more taking it up every year. But the most phenomenal growth in golf is occurring worldwide. Continental Europe, Japan, the nations of the Far East, parts of Latin America and Africa, even Russia, are among those transforming the once-clubbish rich man's pastime into a game of truly international dimensions.

For those people grown accustomed to American dominance in the professional game, this brave new world of multicultural golf must be a trifle unsettling. The years of U.S. monopoly in the Ryder Cup are over. The very best pro players no longer carry American passports exclusively, and unless newcomers such as 1991 PGA wonder boy John Daily, Robert Gamez, the hefty Chris Patton ("That's the only player I ever saw who takes a divot just standing there"—Gary Player), and Phil Mickelson pick up the slack, our reputation as the world's foremost golf power may be in for a terrible drubbing in the coming years.

As unlikely as it may seem now, one of the countries doing the drubbing might be the Soviet Union. The Tumba Golf Club of Moscow, built and organized by a former Swedish ice hockey star, has a 9-hole course, dining rooms, pro shop, and a special club for businesspeople. It's impossible to say if Tumba is the on the edge of a wave in the land of Lenin, or if it's simply a bizarre curiosity. Boris

Yeltsin, president of the Russian Republic, hit the first ball to baptize the new club in the summer of 1990. Predictably, the club is too expensive, and thus off-limits, for the average Russian. But if golf is ever made an Olympic sport and the official Soviet sporting bodies get going on it, in the next decade you might see an elite corps of sharpshooting Russians who can play at a world-class level. But don't hold your breath.

In Japan, golf is likewise an elitist pastime, though what keeps people from playing is not ideology but money. You need money, lots and lots and lots of money, to get into a private club there. At Tokyo's Koganei club the asking price for a new membership begins at $2.5 million—and just because you ask, doesn't mean you'll get in. One applicant reportedly offered Koganei well over $3 million and was turned down flat. For public courses, weekend greens fees run $200 to $300 and up, and you better make your reservation three months ahead of time or you'll be out of luck. It's no wonder that most Japanese golfers have never played on a golf course; their acquaintanceship with the game comes from the driving range, which also demands reservations well in advance.

The world's largest driving range is Shiba Golf in Tokyo. It is three stories of golfers stacked one on top of another hitting balls into a net across a synthetic surface. If you decide you want to get out on a real course, you will encounter crowded conditions far worse than the most horrendous Sunday backup you have ever experienced at the nearby pitch 'n' putt. The average wait between *shots* is ten minutes. After you're done with nine holes you retire to the clubhouse to wait for your tee time for the second nine. Due to the numbers of people playing, Japanese courses start people off on both the front and back nines during the day, making it as difficult to finish a full round as it is to get one started in the first place.

Nor is Japan exactly enlightened on the matter of women and golf. The caddies are nearly all females, the golfers nearly all males. The women caddies uniformly wear hats with a covering that frames and largely obscures their faces. Stooping and fetching, doing all the grunt work on the course, bowing to the orders of the men who employ them, their subservient role is a sorry reflection on the status of women in Japanese society as a whole.

Despite these drawbacks, golf is booming in Japan, one measure of which is the number of stateside golf courses, including Pebble Beach and La Costa, purchased by the Japanese in recent years. Japan hosts its own PGA Tour, the richest in the world after the American PGA. The quality of play, however, is not as high as in the U.S. or on the less lucrative European Tour. Europe and Great Britain, of course, offer the keenest threat to American dominance in tournament golf. Unlike the Japanese, who seldom perform well here, men with names like Faldo, Lyle, Olazabal, Ballesteros, and Langer have shown themselves exceedingly capable of making raids on the treasuries of major domestic golf-o-ramas.

Besides the Japanese, European, and American circuits, many other golf tours around the world offer their own unique challenges. It is in these places, in fact, where one can get a real taste of the wide, wide world of golf.

In Australia, players might encounter a six-foot-wide crack in a fairway in drought-plagued New South Wales, or in Sydney they might step into what they think is a bunker and instead find themselves sinking in quicksand. Africa has the Safari Tour where, as the joke goes, "a good flight is one that lands safely, and a good tournament is one where you don't get food poisoning." The Safari Tour journeys into such nations as Kenya, Nigeria, and Zimbabwe. In Zimbabwe, Nick Price once killed a warthog with a tee shot while playing near Victoria Falls.

Further adventures can be found on the so-called Rice Tour, which travels to Hong Kong, Singapore, Malaysia, the Philippines, and other exotic ports of call. At the Singapore Open one year an American golfer named Jimmy Stewart killed a ten-foot-long cobra with a 3-iron after encountering the snake curled up in his bag.

Another Stewart, name of Payne, was in a foursome in New Delhi when a member of his party lofted a ball over the green and then went to look for it in the bushes. He came flying out again after a king cobra, fully erect, had raised up at him preparing to strike. "He decided to drop a ball," recalls Payne.

Snakes are common on the Rice Tour. So are umbrellas. They're a necessity to keep off the intense heat. Rain is also a constant threat. A sudden monsoon, coupled with lightning, can turn a fairway into a flood plain in a matter of minutes. In these types of conditions you learn to be resourceful, and in this regard you have to hand it to tournament officials at a recent Malaysian Open. They hired a medicine man, or *bomoh,* to keep the rain away during the course of the event. The *bomoh* took up a position on the 18th fairway and spun spells for four days—four dry, wonderfully mild days. And not a half hour after the last competitor left the final green ending the tournament, observers swear that the skies opened up and poured rain. With talents like that, that *bomoh* could probably find a job at several major stateside resorts.

America's Favorite Australian

Greg Norman has replaced Crocodile Dundee as America's favorite Australian, although since Norman is now living in Florida, he may be becoming America's favorite ex-Australian. We like Norman because he is big and blond and a hunk, because he's a man's man, and because he loses in the most wonderfully extravagant ways. This last quality Norman would just as soon do without, though it has helped make him wealthy and famous.

Norman has a lovely wife and lovely children. When he tires of the domestic life, he has a garage full of Ferraris and Aston Martins with which to escape. He also drives Grand Prix racing cars and flies jets and dreams of someday landing an F-16 fighter on an aircraft carrier. He is a certified scuba diver and has ventured down in a cage into the waters off Australia and bumped noses (so to speak) with great white sharks. With a little help from his friends, the Shark, a deep-sea fisherman, has himself bagged a shark weighing over half a ton.

Norman is and does all of this and more, so isn't it a bit . . . *odd* that when it comes to golf all we can talk about is what a big loser he is?

He lost the 1989 British Open in a playoff. He lost the 1987 Masters in a playoff when somebody named Larry Mize holed a 140-foot chip. At the 1986 PGA Championship, Bob "Who?" Tway knocked in a bunker shot on the final hole to deprive him of victory. That same year Norman led all of the majors after three rounds, but only came away with a win at the British. He has been shark-bit in the lesser tournaments as well, losing on a fifty-foot sand shot by David Frost on the last hole at the New Orleans Classic and an eagle from the fairway by Robert Gamez at the Bay Hill Classic, both of which occurred in 1990, a year in which Norman, nevertheless, ended up as the tour's leading money-winner.

In the pressroom following such hard-to-swallow defeats, Norman has become accustomed to making generous-spirited concession speeches:

"What can you say? He hit a great shot. I'm out there trying to win, and he's out there trying to win. Just 'well done' to him. You just try to be as philosophical as you can about it." (After the Frost defeat.)

"Sometimes you play bad golf and win. Sometimes you play great golf and lose. Because of the way things ended up, people forgot what I had created that day. I had painted this beautiful picture and I didn't win. You paint a picture like that, you still have to walk away with your head up." (After the British Open playoff loss in which he shot a final-round 64.)

"There's nothing I can do about it. It's passed. It's history. If I thought about it, I'd probably be in a funny farm now." (On his losses in general.)

This is, of course, one of the reasons we like Greg Norman. He gets knocked down, he gets up, he shakes the winner's hand, and he goes on. Nobody likes a sore loser. Nobody likes a whiner, especially when, as is so often the case in professional sports, the person doing the whining is a millionaire jock who's never worked a straight job in his life. The Jose Cansecos and Eric Dickersons of this world could learn a thing or two from the Shark. But this is not to confuse good sportsmanship with passivity. Norman is no wimp—and this is another reason we like him. At a U.S. Open some years ago at Shinnecock Hills, Norman double-bogeyed the 13th hole, at which time a drunk fan called out, "You're choking, you white-haired bastard!" Norman turned immediately and strode over to the gallery ropes where he confronted the man: "If you have something to say to me, wait until after the round when I can do something about it." The drunk shut his trap.

Another time one of the touring pros said some unkind words about Norman that were duly noted by the ink-stained wretches of the press. When the object of these criticisms saw the pro at a tournament the following week, he escorted him over to a quiet corner in the clubhouse. "Hey, you want a piece of me or something?" Norman demanded. The pro, perhaps recognizing that the man whose face was pressed up against his had lately developed an intimate acquaintanceship with sharks, said he did not, and the public hectoring of Norman in the press ceased.

Nor is Norman hesitant at confronting legends, if the situation demands it. Arnold Palmer happened to be in the locker room at Bay Hill the day Robert Gamez airmailed in the longest winning fairway shot on a final hole in PGA history. When the loser walked in afterward, Palmer jokingly told him to get away, that he was bad luck and Arnold didn't want any of it rubbing off on him. This did not sit too well with Mr. Norman, who reacted with harsh words. Both men later apologized to each other.

Norman is not a hothead. But he comes from a country, as Jerry Tarde has noted, "where the fistfight is considered a recreational sport," and he does stand up for himself. Who can fault him for that?

Another thing we like about Norman is the way he plays the game. He can really powder the ball. "I don't think he hits the ball quite as far relative to the other players as I did," says Jack Nicklaus, who once designated Norman to be heir to the throne formerly occupied by Jack. "We have more big, strong players today than when I was growing up. I grew up in the era of the Finsterwalds and Heberts, guys who played placement golf. I went out and just knocked it over everything. Norman does the same thing."

In the late 1960s Augusta National built some fairway bunkers about 300 yards from the tee, with the aim of handicapping Nicklaus's long game. But at a Masters a few years ago Norman's tee ball carried those bunkers, rendering them obsolete. Sometimes, though, all that power has gotten him into trouble. At the 1989 British Open at Royal Troon, Norman, Mark Calcavecchia, and Wayne Grady competed in a four-hole playoff. After taking a tough bogey on the third playoff hole (the 17th, on the course), Norman was tied with Calcavecchia as they approached the last hole. Norman wanted to do something big off the tee, and he certainly did—hitting a colossal 325-yard drive that landed in a bunker so far away that none of the other pros had reached it all week. Faced with a horrible lie on the lip of the bunker, Norman's out put him into another bunker, and he picked up and watched as Calcavecchia got the claret jug.

Norman's shotmaking choices on the finishing holes of the major tournaments have drawn criticism. They're too risky, too imprudent, say some. But unquestionably, this is part of the Norman appeal, too. "He's always right on the edge," says television commentator Jack Whittaker. "Always on the attack. Perhaps that's why he's lost some of the ones he's lost. But it's also why you can't ever take your eyes off him." In the grand Palmer tradition he will not play conservatively, will not suddenly become timid simply because he is approaching the end of the tournament. Caution is fine when directing little children across a busy street. But we demand something more from our heroes. Norman seems to understand this.

The unofficial title of "world's best golfer" passed from Norman to Britain's Nick Faldo on a sunny day in St. Andrews, Scotland, in 1990. Tied after two rounds in the British Open, Norman and Faldo were paired together for the third round. There was talk of great things to come, possibly a duel on the order of the Watson-Nicklaus drama at Turnberry more than a decade before. But while Faldo was carving up the course with a 67 on his way to winning the Open, Norman blew to a 76, losing not only a shot at the title but some prestige as well.

Nonetheless, we like Greg in a way we shall never like the stoical Faldo and all too many of his blank-faced peers, and this has less to do with the way they play golf and more with the unquantifiable fact of charisma, which Norman possesses in spades. Playing in a practice round at a U.S. Open in Brookline, he hit a wedge out of the rough to about twenty feet from the pin. That may have impressed some people, but not the man in the gallery who said, "That shot wasn't so hard." Overhearing the remark, Norman challenged him, "Okay, expert. You come out here and try it." The man in the gallery was named Bruce Charles, a thirty-seven-year-old six-handicapper from a nearby Massachusetts town. Charles set up and using Norman's wedge, hit the ball six feet from the pin. The Australian laughed and applauded along with everyone else, and congratulated Charles with an enthusiastic high five.

The Greatest
Golf Shot Ever Made

The greatest golf shot ever made was not Sarazen's double eagle, although that was pretty close. The greatest golf shot ever made was Tom Watson's chip from the rough to win the 1982 U.S. Open, and here are the reasons why:

1. The ball went in. If it had not gone in, it would still have been a great shot—Watson's lie was horrendous—but it would not have been the best ever. To earn this lofty distinction a golf shot must fulfill a number of criteria, but first and foremost, it must go in the cup. A controversial requirement, to be sure, for it eliminates all drives and long iron shots, all recoveries and approaches that may have come close but did not go in. The game of golf has been filled with such shots—indeed, it is very nearly defined by such shots: and in a round played to the hilt, when you're staying on the fairways and managing the course well and hitting the ball right, getting the ball in the hole becomes a kind of afterthought. What's great about golf is not the end result, it's the getting there.

Nevertheless, the best-ever shot can't just get close; it has to go in. It must be consummated. It must succeed, utterly and conclusively, leaving nothing to chance. For, as has been shown over and over, even a one-foot putt in a pressure environment can be difficult to make. No, this is vital: it has to seal the deal. Watson's chip went in. But so did Sarazen's double eagle. We go on.

2. Both Sarazen's and Watson's master strokes occurred in major tournaments, Sarazen's at the 1935 Masters and Watson's at the Open. This is another fundamental requirement. Paul Azinger may win the Greater Hartford Open with a stunning chip-in birdie on the 72nd

hole. Nice shot, nice guy, nice payday. But it cannot qualify as the ultimate golf shot because it did not occur during a major. The same goes for a Robert Gamez eagle over water on the final hole of the Bay Hill Classic. A great shot alone is not enough; it must occur in the proper context. These days, the most meaningful golf tournaments are the Masters, the U.S. Open, the British Open, and to a declining extent, the PGA Championship.

A corollary requirement is that (3) the greatest shot must occur on a great golf course, one that offers challenging conditions as well as a sense of history and tradition. No one can doubt that both Augusta National and Pebble Beach satisfy this rule easily.

The greatest shot must be made on a great course in a great tournament, and (4) it must come at a crucial time in the match and significantly affect its outcome. This shot cannot take place in a preliminary round; it must occur on the fourth, and final, round. But we must narrow our focus still further. The front nine is not appropriate, for dramatic reasons. Everything must be riding on the shot. The chances to make up ground later in the round must all have been winnowed away. That leaves the 18th as the best possible hole for the shot to take place, with the 17th next, and so on down the back nine in corresponding order.

Rule No. 5 might be called the Bob Tway rule. As Tway showed at the 1986 PGA, sometimes it happens that a person comes out of nowhere, makes the shot of his life, and wins a major tournament. In Tway's case, he holed a shot out of a bunker to win. This, however, does not qualify because (5) the greatest shot must be performed by an acknowledged great player. (Sorry Bob, that leaves you out, but don't feel too bad. Only fifteen or twenty players in the last one hundred years even qualify.) The reason for this is to eliminate all chances of a fluke or a lucky break. The best-ever shot must be an expression of a game—and a golfer—that has proven itself in the major tournaments over a period of time.

Both Watson and Sarazen have honored seats in the throne room of golf's immortals. One of the very best players of the twenties and thirties, Sarazen won two U.S. Opens, one British Open, three PGAs, and a Masters. Watson, the best player of his generation, can see Sarazen and raise him with two Masters, one U.S. Open, and five British Opens. Only four people have accumulated more majors than Watson's eight, and Sarazen is just a notch behind.

But a great player making a great shot is not sufficient unto itself; (6) he must beat an all-time great player as well. Again, context is all. Greatness demands greatness. Ali needed Frazier; the '75 Reds needed Boston; Achilles needed Hector. The greatest-ever shot must occur in a match with nothing less at stake than the kingdom of golfing heaven. This, finally, is what separates Watson's chip from all the others, including Sarazen's.

Sarazen hit his colossal double eagle—a 265-yard 4-wood from the fairway—on the 15th hole at Augusta. It's widely but mistakenly believed that it occurred on the 18th and won him the tournament on the spot. In fact, what it did was earn him a tie after regulation with Craig Wood, whom he later beat in a playoff. Wood was a fine player in his day, but someone who was best known for the tournaments he almost won rather than the ones he did.

Watson's opponent, in contrast, was Jack Nicklaus, whose credentials need hardly to be recited here. The best golfer of his generation against the best of all time—now *that's* golf. What's more, Nicklaus and Watson had a history together; they had tangled head-to-head in a number of tournaments over the years, most notably the 1977 Masters and the 1977 British Open, both of which were won by Watson in supremely exciting and well-played matches.

Watson's birdie two also met the next requirement for a best-ever shot, which is (7) it has to beat par. In golf, par is regulation, the prescribed number of shots for playing a given hole. This is not to say there haven't been plenty of heroic pars. One thinks of Lee Trevino's chip on the 71st hole of the 1972 British Open, which enabled him to beat Nicklaus and Tony Jacklin in one of the best golf matches ever played. That wondrous wedge won Trevino the tournament, no question. But in terms of the hole itself, it only saved par—achieved the standard. A birdie or better, on the other hand, signifies success in relation to the golf course, which is, after all, the last, best test for every golfer.

The 209-yard 17th at Pebble Beach points straight at Carmel Bay, and the winds blowing in off the Pacific Ocean make it one of the hardest par 3s in all of golf. Ironically, one of Nicklaus's best-ever shots occurred there: a tremendous 1-iron into the wind that hit the flag, settling down inches away for a birdie putt that sealed his 1972 U.S. Open win. Watson's tee ball on 17 was nothing of this order and put him in deep, deep trouble. Tied for the lead with Nicklaus, who was in the clubhouse, as he sized up his second shot, Watson knew he had to do something great . . . *now!*

Born and raised in Missouri, Watson is a Stanford University graduate who had to overcome the label of "choker" after blowing some big tournaments early in his career. He won the 1975 British Open, but it was not until the Masters two years later, when he held off a Nicklaus charge on the final round, that he really arrived as a major golf player. And then for a few years after that he was unstoppable. Although he has mellowed in recent years, he was seen by his fellow pros as intense, ambitious, competitive. Not particularly charismatic, he seldom said a word on the golf course. But he had enormous confidence in himself, and when his caddie, surveying his lie on 17, said, "Just get it close," Watson looked him straight in the eye and told him, "I'm going to chip it in."

Those who saw Watson's chip judged it to be a 10,000-to-1 shot. His ball was in deep rough on the left side of a green that was "slicker than tile," in Dan Jenkins's words. The ball had to roll downhill toward the hole. After the tournament was over, Bill Rogers, Watson's partner for the day, told him, "You could hit that chip shot a hundred times and you couldn't get it close to the pin, much less in the hole." But Watson disagreed. "I've practiced that shot for hours, days, months, years," he said. Fittingly, the best-ever golf shot was born out of strength; Watson, a fine wedge player, hit a sand wedge.

But craft alone cannot make for the greatest-ever shot; it must contain—and this is the eighth, and final, requirement—a piece of the sublime. It must be a sort of miracle. We're not talking luck here—this is more on the order of providence. That chip shot simply had to go in, there was no other choice for it, and after destiny had had its say Watson was champion.

Index

ABOUT THE AUTHOR

Kevin Nelson is the author of five books on sports.
He started playing golf three years ago,
and like so many others, he is now addicted to the game.
He lives with his artist-wife and daughter in the
San Francisco Bay Area.